D1756620

Please return/renew this item by the last date shown. Books may also be renewed by phone or internet.

🖥 www.rbwm.gov.uk/home/leisure-and-culture/libraries

☎ 01628 796969 (library hours)

☎ 0303 123 0035 (24 hours)

Windsor and Maidenhead

95800000217799

The Secret Life of a
WOODLAND HABITAT

Life Through the Seasons

CHLOÉ VALERIE HARMSWORTH

WHITE OWL

AN IMPRINT OF PEN & SWORD BOOKS LTD.
YORKSHIRE – PHILADELPHIA

First published in Great Britain in 2022 by
White Owl
An imprint of
Pen & Sword Books Ltd
Yorkshire - Philadelphia

ISBN 978 1 39909 334 7

A CIP catalogue record for this book is available from the British Library.

Typeset in 11/14 pts Cormorant Infant
by SJmagic DESIGN SERVICES, India.
Printed and bound in India by Replika Press Pvt. Ltd.

Pen & Sword Books Ltd incorporates the imprints of Pen & Sword Books Archaeology, Atlas, Aviation, Battleground, Discovery, Family History, History, Maritime, Military, Naval, Politics, Railways, Select, Transport, True Crime, Fiction, Frontline Books, Leo Cooper, Praetorian Press, Seaforth Publishing, Wharncliffe and White Owl.

For a complete list of Pen & Sword titles please contact

PEN & SWORD BOOKS LIMITED
47 Church Street, Barnsley, South Yorkshire, S70 2AS, England
E-mail: enquiries@pen-and-sword.co.uk
Website: www.pen-and-sword.co.uk

or

PEN AND SWORD BOOKS
1950 Lawrence Rd, Havertown, PA 19083, USA
E-mail: Uspen-and-sword@casematepublishers.com
Website: www.penandswordbooks.com

Contents

Credits

All photography (including cover) © Chloé Valerie Harmsworth
Except for hedgehog & badger © Nick Wilson-Smith
Forage Walk poem © Stefan Peter Glosby
Spring, Summer and Autumn poems © Chloé Valerie Harmsworth

Foreword

Woodlands are very special places, and the Woodland Trust is lucky enough to own and manage a large number of them. Many are iconic, celebrated for the age of their trees, the nature they hold and the atmosphere they create. Many are local and celebrated by the community as a place to visit to recharge the batteries. Due to the Covid pandemic, there has been a heightened awareness of just how important local woodlands are for the nation's physical and mental well-being. That connecting with nature helps us to cope with the stresses and strains of everyday life. I have been fortunate to appreciate this ever since I was a youngster.

I first met Chloé during one of my first visits to the Woodland Trust's Heartwood Forest. I had recently been given the privilege to be made Chief Executive of the Trust – the UK's largest woodland conservation charity – and I was meeting the local group of expert volunteers who had been (and remain) instrumental to the forest's success. That success is a special place covering 858 acres, made up of ancient woodland blocks buffered by over 600,000 trees planted by volunteers, as well as areas of naturally regenerated woodland and open wildflower meadows.

Despite over 20 years working in the conservation sector, I'm not ashamed to say that there are still many people who know a great deal more than me about the myriad species that you may encounter when out in nature. Walking in the woods is an uplifting experience – whatever the season, whatever the weather. It may be the woodpecker drumming or the enchanting song of a warbler, the munching of a beetle, the scent of the ground flora, or simply the wind through the trees or a drop in temperature under the canopy.

For me, the woodland experience is always made that little more special by knowing which woodpecker, which beetle. Through her writing, Chloé helps readers to appreciate the natural world around them, heightening their senses to notice more, enjoy more and, in doing so, benefit more from a deeper connection with nature.

Darren Moorcroft
Chief Executive of the Woodland Trust

Acknowledgements

As with any species within a woodland ecosystem, this book would not have come into being without essential input, support and help from others.

The humans I'd like to thank are as follows:

Amy Burgess, for our restorative nature walks of 2020 and 2021; Rose and Dave Newbold, for the kind use of their cameras; Tegwen Edmonds, for the emergency use of her camera; Claudia Harflett, for the excellent research trips!

Thanks also to Darren Moorcroft for his Foreword, my fellow Heartwood Forest volunteers for caring about woodlands and wildlife, and Eleri Pipien, Jonathan Wright and the teams at Newgen Publishing UK and White Owl for giving me the wonderful opportunity to write this book.

My heartfelt appreciation goes to my amazing friends, the nature-loving community on Instagram, my parents and parents-in-law, and – of course – my husband, Stefan Glosby. Without his constant belief, love and encouragement, it is unlikely that I would be following my dream.

Beyond these special humans, my eternal gratitude goes to the trees, birds and magical creatures that delight and inspire me daily – especially those inhabiting my local woodlands and fields. I know that without you, I would not exist. I hope that I can give back at least half of what you give to me.

Chloé Valerie Harmsworth
Nature writer, photographer and artist

chloevalerienatureart.wordpress.com / Instagram @chloevalerienatureart / Twitter @ChloeValerieNA

Introduction

Why this book is for you

This book is for you if you love nature and want to get to know it better. It's for you if you long to gain an understanding of the wonderful wildlife that can be found in our woodlands and find out what the furred and feathered cast of characters are up to during the four seasons. It's for you if you'd like to start putting names to the majestic trees, attractive wildflowers and fascinating fungi of the woodland. It's for you if you're curious about the tiny insects that live there. And it's also for you if you wish to deepen your awareness of the role all of these play in the delicate ecosystem of this unique and valuable environment.

I've written this guide to help you recognise and appreciate how precious our woodlands are, with details about the beguiling creatures that call them home, and the individual aspects of various trees. I focus on broadleaved woodlands as the most original and natural to the UK, although some of the species I mention can be found in coniferous forests too.

The main chapters are separated by the seasons, with the intention being that you can open the book to whichever season you are in, and identify examples of things to look out for when you go on your next walk. Each season is split into the following categories: trees and plants; wildflowers; birds; insects; mammals. This way the content of each should be clear and accessible, to better give you direction on your own journey of discovery. My wish is that you feel emboldened by my words to engage with the little details in nature and keep your eyes open for the many miracles residing amongst the trunks, leaves, grass, brambles and bracken around you. To add extra flavour, I've dropped in bits of folklore here and there, to demonstrate how our relationship with the woodlands has changed over the course of human history.

Ultimately, I want to increase the value of these special places within your mind and heart, so that you feel inspired to conserve and protect them, and spread the word about how vital it is that we do so. The majority of society has become disconnected from nature – the result being that our woodlands are disappearing, wildlife species are in rapid decline, and human physical and mental well-being is suffering.

The truth of the matter is that woodlands, and therefore we, are in a dire situation; however it is my belief that it doesn't take long to re-forge our relationship with nature. The reason we find a bird or a tree beautiful is because deep down we realise that we are also a part of nature, that it is essential to us and our future. Plus we experience joy in the presence of abundance and variety, and we do not aspire to live in an empty and mundane world. By celebrating the wonders and exquisiteness of our woodlands, we will not only reconnect with nature; we will learn what we need to do to save it and become determined to alter the catastrophic course that we are on.

After working your way through the seasons and falling fully in love with woodlands and their wildlife, turn to the end of the book for further information and inspiration, including two excellent examples of planting and rewilding projects, as well as suggestions and resources to help you join the rescue mission.

Bluebell woodland.

The woodland environment and ecosystem

Here I'd like to give you an overview of why UK woodland is so essential to our world.

As an environment, broadleaved woodlands are potentially the most diverse habitat in the UK, being home to an extensive range of plants, insects, birds and other animals. They are our equivalent of the Amazon rainforest. When compared to the other types of environment on this island, their ecological benefits are wide-ranging, far-reaching and unparalleled. And yet, together with their tropical counterparts, our woodlands are continually decreasing in size and variation to such an extent that an enormous number of organisms are becoming extinct, or soon will be.

The ecosystem of the broadleaved woodland is formed of complex, interrelated food webs in a delicate network of interdependence. If one species suffers serious decline or becomes extinct (locally or nationally) due to habitat loss or lack of food, the whole food web is impacted in a disastrous domino-effect. Without plants and flowers, there can be no insects. Without insects, the birds and the rest of the animals will starve.

THE SECRET LIFE OF A WOODLAND HABITAT

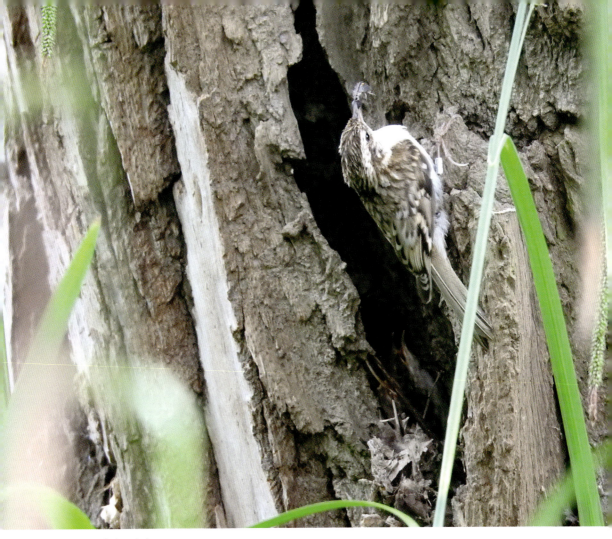

Treecreeper feeding chicks.

As a result of the national and international destruction of woodlands and forests, the world's ecosystem is breaking down, thus dissolving the structure that makes life sustainable. Relying on this planet as much any other animal – a part of this global ecosystem – we are likewise endangered: our survival is also at stake.

Not only is there less plant life and wildlife in our world, but we've altered and obstructed the ways in which our planet works. By systematically cutting down our woodlands to replace them with nature-poor environments such as farmland, houses, cities and monoculture plantations (for example, for timber), we do not have the necessary number of trees to capture the carbon that is changing our climate. Our foolhardy pursuit of 'progress' and wealth has led to processes that damage our environment, and a build-up of toxic chemicals and pollutants that have caused our weather systems to change and our seasons to shift.

Mild winters mean that insects can emerge early, misaligned with the species that rely on them or that they rely on. For example, caterpillars may be in abundance weeks before the birth of the newborn birds that require them to survive and thrive, and bees may cease hibernation to search for nectar from flowers that have not yet opened. The latter would mean that fewer plants' flowers would be pollinated – impacting food production for humans and other animals.

In addition to being aware of the impact that losing our pollinators and wildlife will have on our future – food shortages and so on – we must remember that trees are the crucial factor in whether life, as it currently exists on earth, will continue or not. Which is why discarding them is equivalent to destroying ourselves. Without them, as temperatures rise, where would be the trees to shelter us? As floods rage, where would be the trees to hold back their flow? As the soil erodes, where would be the trees to hold it, and therefore our world, together? And without trees to produce our oxygen, how will we breathe?

Considering how vital woodlands have been to humans over the course of our history, it is surprising that we have let it get to this point. These are the places we originally lived in, sheltered in and hunted in. We foraged their fruits and used their timber to build houses, churches, carts and ships to explore the world in. It was where we used to let our pigs and cattle graze. Initially, it was a reasonably symbiotic and sustainable relationship; however, as our population expanded and industrialisation followed, the woodland has been corrupted, exploited, undervalued and, by many, forgotten. The UK is now one of the least wooded countries in Europe and one of the most nature-depleted countries in the world.

But there is no use in just accepting how things are. There are many organisations striving to improve matters, for the benefit of all. You can join forces with them, or find other ways to make a difference. More detail on this is provided towards the end of this book. But first, begin by re-establishing your sense of wonder and awe in the presence of nature, and by building upon your relationship with your local woodland.

Why woodlands matter to me

I have loved woodlands and animals since I was a child. The house I grew up in was close to a field bordered by a meadow that had patches of woodland surrounding it. For hours on end, I played outside in the fresh air and in dens I discovered beneath the hawthorn and blackthorn bushes. It was a medium-sized green space on the edge of an urban town – we weren't part of the proper rural countryside – but the environment certainly enriched my childhood.

I also planted trees there – part of a community project – and living in the area again many years later, I am amazed by how much they have grown. Where there had been a small row of trees right next to the meadow, there is now a full-blown woodland.

But, before I came back, I (like many) lost my connection to nature. Life – the way I was told it should be – got in the way. And I wasn't happy. My mental health suffered. It wasn't until I became self-employed that I had time and motivation to commit to my relationship with nature again.

Initially I began by volunteering at Heartwood Forest, helping to clear brambles and plant trees. Then I started going even when there weren't work parties, to wander and sit in the forest (and sometimes sketch and write). It helped me through a difficult time trapped in a place I didn't belong; in the woodlands at Heartwood I was able to find a long-lost sense of home, calm and peace. Years passed, but eventually I made it back to where I had grown up. It was spring, and the start of my new, more fulfilling life. A life in which my connection with nature began to deepen and flourish.

It is my belief that, because our lifestyles have taken the majority of us away from nature, this is why the world is in its current predicament. Even on a small scale, most of us are not part of a community that reveres nature and realises how we rely on it to sustain life. As we spend most of our time inside, we have lost our understanding of the seasons and how nature works. We don't notice the signs that indicate how our world is transforming. This disconnect leaves us disorientated and feeling as if we are missing something – because we are. Our lifestyles are not conducive to physical and mental well-being.

Bee drinking nectar from white dead-nettle.

For the last few years, I have been keeping a nature diary of my local woodlands. This keeps me in tune with the seasons and the weather, as well as what I can see, when I can see it, and why. By seeing it, relating to it and understanding it, the world makes more sense to me and I feel more myself than ever before. I encounter my sense of belonging in nature, especially in the woodlands.

John Ruskin believed that by becoming absorbed in nature, in all its unbounded, unspoiled, awe-inspiring magnificence, we can bring about a form of self-healing, and increase our human contentment. In his 1870s 'Grammars' books, he encouraged people to engage in the natural world, as he was convinced that looking closely and naming and studying nature leads to a wholeness of being and brings about an attitude of reverence and respect. And the best thing about nature is that it is for everyone, no matter their background or experience: 'Nature paints for all the world, poor and rich together' (*The Two Paths lectures*, 1859). I certainly think we could do with following his ideas in this modern, detached world.

Nature accepts you, whoever you are. By spending time in it, you will relieve any worries or anxieties you may have. You will make memories that are yours and nature's alone. By grounding yourself in nature, in your own woodland, you will find an inner strength and resilience that will aid you in all aspects of your life. And I hope that you will be filled with a desire to protect your woodland – that gives you so much – as well as others across the UK.

Tips and advice before you step into the woodland

To get the most out of your forays into the woodland, I recommend you take a few things with you:

1. Binoculars
2. A notebook and pen
3. A camera

The first two are the most important. Binoculars will get you closer to wildlife without disturbing it. Hear a bird high up in a tree? With binoculars, you can locate it and see it up close. See a deer in the distance? Use the binoculars to discern which type of deer you are looking at.

The notebook is a good way to consolidate your learning: write down the date, what you see and where. You can then remind yourself of your sightings when you get home, refer to this book for more information, and even carry out further research on the things that particularly interest you (I've listed some useful websites and books in the 'Resources' section at the back). By doing this, you will build up a picture of the unique elements of your woodland and become familiar with its residents and their mysterious ways.

The third item is a bonus, particularly if you want to have images to confirm your identification of plants and creatures at a later date. However, it doesn't have to be a fancy camera if this is all you are using it for, a simple camera phone will suffice in many cases. It's worth being aware that often, it isn't easy to take photos of animals no matter how good your equipment is. Especially when it comes to mammals. Birds can hear you and see you, but mammals can also smell you coming from a mile off. So your view of them will usually be brief but magical. Insects and butterflies are also flighty by nature. Make the most of the seconds you are granted by taking the view in with your own eyes – that is more memorable than missing it while fiddling with your camera. Once you have built your knowledge and relationship, then by all means, snap away. But don't forget to relish nature for its own sake too. Take it from me, it's all too easy to become focused on getting the perfect image and losing sight of appreciating the moment itself. That said, if you use Instagram, feel free to tag me @chloevalerienatureart, as I'd love to see what you discover!

On that note, although this book aims to develop your knowledge and understanding of trees, wildflowers, birds, insects and mammals, and give you the confidence to continue the journey yourself, I urge you to bear in mind that you do not need to know everything to appreciate nature. You cannot know everything anyway. Furthermore, as much as you can get a lot from visiting various woodlands around the UK, there is a lot to be said for focusing your efforts purely on one or two woodlands. I suspect that this is the best way to understand woodlands as a whole – by knowing one really well. The innovative eighteenth century parson-naturalist

Woodland entrance.

Gilbert White, who kept records of his local nature for over forty years, saw 'new beauties' that filled him with 'fresh admiration' all the time. And when it came to his favourite subject – birds – he was never able to 'exhaust the subject'.

As much as I want you to connect with all of the wonderful things in your woodland, please also respect the environment and the wildlife that calls it home. Do your best not to disturb animals or get too friendly or close. Animals need to stay wild so that they do not end up being too trusting of humans, which unfortunately will generally lead to their downfall. Remember that some animals are nocturnal, so you may have to satisfy yourself with simply knowing that they exist in the woodland – although you may find footprints or other fascinating signs of their presence! Don't forget to take your litter away with you, and leave things where they are supposed to be. Leave no human impression except for your footprints.

Finally, please enjoy this book and your future adventures in nature!

CHAPTER 1

Winter

'...deep down among the roots of the earth all small beasts were sleeping
and dreaming of spring.'

Moominland Midwinter by Tove Jansson

Introduction

Winter brings with it visions of cold, grey and quiet days that are better spent indoors. Days without much to offer the nature-lover or enthusiast. Yet in reality, the woodlands are full of colour, activity, song, sound and beauty. It is also the easiest time of year to watch birds and learn to identify trees, as the lack of leaves means that our feathered friends are less obscured, and the buds and bark of the bare trees can be studied. With the aid of binoculars, plus bird and tree identification guides, you can learn to distinguish your redwing from your song thrush, and figure out your ash from your alder.

As you crunch across crackly grass and leaves, hardened mud and frozen puddles, both your physical and mental well-being will improve. The fresh air and exercise are invigorating and will clear your mind of heavy thoughts and rid your body of fatigue. Even on slate-grey days you will get a vital boost of Vitamin D and discover the treasures of this magical and underrated season. And on foggy days, the woodland is transformed into an eerie, atmospheric, fairy-tale place.

On sunny, frosty days, the whole woodland is encrusted with sparkling ice that is lit up by the sun to stunning effect. The lichen-covered blackthorn shines silver in the light and dogwood bushes glow with bright red or yellow-green stems. Once you have witnessed what is one of the most beautiful sights of the year, you will wonder what else you have been missing.

By embracing the elements and rhythms of winter, you will truly be living life to its fullest. Finding joy in everything big or small, whatever the weather, will make you feel more alive than ever before. On a wet and windy woodland walk, you may be rewarded with an encounter with a mouse, a glimpse of the secretive treecreeper, and the creaking song of the swaying trees.

You will realise that, when you look closely, there are undeniable signs that spring is approaching: golden hazel catkins swinging in the breeze; green shoots pushing up from the damp ground; snowdrops appearing on the woodland floor. Likewise, the tree buds are swelling and growing, preparing to burst open with new flowers and leaves when spring arrives.

Moreover, winter can be a time of planning for the forthcoming seasons. Here's a poem written by my husband, Stefan Glosby, which illustrates how winter is the ideal time for exploring and discovering the trees and plants in your local woodland, with future foraging in mind:

Hazel catkins in the snow.

Forage Walk – by Stefan Glosby

Ambling through the nearby wood
Crunchy puddles underfoot
Taking stock of what grows where
Jotting it down in our notebook

Wrapped up warm in coats and scarves
Holding hands in gloves
Flask of coffee in my bag
And a little pair of mugs

Last year's berries cling to branches
Oak galls scatter on the ground
A great tit's rusty gate-like song
The only audible sound

We write it all down and find somewhere to sit
Get out the flask and have a drink
Taking in the frozen peace
A chance to sit and stop and think

'We've got some sloe berries in the freezer
And a small bottle of gin
We can get an infusion on the go
It'll be ready in time for spring'

The sky begins to darken
So we pack up and depart
Looking forward to the year's first forage
And impatient to start.

Trees, bushes and plants

With the majority of woodland foliage now out of the way, you can inspect the buds of a tree – which goes a long way towards helping you to identify it. This can then be backed up by studying the patterns of the bark and the overall shape of the tree. Later, in spring and summer, you will be able to fully confirm your identification by observing the flowers, leaves and fruit of the same tree. It is incredibly satisfying to do so – to know the trees in your woodland.

Ash

The tall and elegant ash tree is one of the simplest trees to identify. Its twigs end with three distinctive matt black buds, shaped like pointed hooves. They are unlike the buds of any other tree. The tree's bark is smooth and silvery, and sometimes speckled with white like a fawn's side. Its leaves are similar to those of the rowan tree, but much less serrated.

In spring, you will notice clusters of purple flowers exploding from the ash buds, and by the end of summer, you will see groups of singular seeds or 'keys' hanging from the branches. These keys quite often stay on the branches long after the leaves have fallen, aiding your identification of the ash in winter.

The ash tree has always been of great importance to humans, serving a variety of essential purposes alongside our development as a society. A solid and smooth wood that is easy to work with, and without multiple knots, ash wood has been used from our very beginning to make axes, arrows and wheels, and in recent times to make high-quality furniture and cricket bats.

Some pagan mythologies describe humans as descendants of the ash tree, and the Scandinavian World Tree (which supported the entire universe) was said to be an ash. In Norse mythology, the Gods created the first man (named Askr) by breathing a human soul into an ash. From Askr and his female companion (who was made from an alder tree), all the people of the world were said to be descended.

Unfortunately, ash trees are susceptible to ash dieback. A fungal disease that has come from imported ash trees, ash dieback is fast spreading through Britain, leaving skeletal trees in its wake. The Sylva Foundation estimates that the disease, first discovered in 2012, will kill up to 95–98% of our native ash trees.

Goldfinch eating ash keys.

The Woodland Trust says there isn't much we can do to halt the spread of the disease and the full impact is not yet known. As a nation, we will probably need to plant a lot of other trees to make up for this devastating loss. Research is currently being carried out into ash trees in Europe which appear to be immune, and resistant genes have been identified. Hopefully this will mean that new ash trees, not susceptible to the disease, can be bred. Whatever the long-term answer is, let's hope that we can avoid the ash tree being remembered by name alone: in place names such as Ashby-de-la-Zouch and Ashton-under-Lyne, and in forenames such as Ashley or Ashleigh.

Ash buds and keys.

English oak

There are over 600 species of oak worldwide. Ones found in the UK include the turkey oak, red oak, cypress oak, holm oak and cork oak (the bark of which is used to make the cork in your wine bottle) – but it is the English oak (*Quercus robur*) and the Sessile oak (*Quercus petraea*) that are our two main species. Due to its majesty and very long life, the English oak (also known as the Pedunculate oak) has become a symbol of all things English, representing the country's rich heritage. This is why both the Woodland Trust and the National Trust use the English oak's instantly-recognisable leaves in their logos. Once you recognise the shape of oak leaves, with their deep, rounded lobes and smooth edges, it is hard to confuse them with any others – except for those of other oak trees, of course!

The buds of this grand tree are surprisingly unassuming: small, pointy and reddish-pink. They appear in a cluster at end of a twig, with single ones alternating along the rest of the twig. Two other trees have similar buds: the beech (although these are thinner and longer) and the cherry (although comparing the bark will help you to tell the two apart – see the cherry section later on).

The bark of the oak is rough, with wavy vertical ridges. Oaks grow to a very impressive size in both height and girth, and possess characterful twisted branches, some of which descend to the ground as the tree ages. In very old oaks, daughter trees can sprout from branches that have re-entered the soil.

In spring, the oak's subtle catkins will appear as delicate yellow-green strands amongst the leaves. In autumn, the familiar acorns will remove any remaining doubts.

The oak has been a special tree in our woodlands ever since it was worshipped by druids and pagans. Folk tales say that it is unlucky to cut down an oak tree, and that you will be cursed if you do. And yet, not only has the oak's enormous limbs inspired the architecture of cathedrals, but its strong wood has helped to build them too. This revered material wasn't just used for the house of god, though – everyday people's houses were built using it. The wood was used by Vikings for their warships, and the other ships that sailed out to protect England or discover new lands, since oak bark is resistant to rotting. Other uses for the bark included tanning leather and fixing dye colours onto cloth. Today, it is the preferred material for barrels, imparting its earthy flavours into alcohols such as whisky, sherry and wine.

The oak tree is essential for our wildlife, providing a habitat for more organisms than any other tree in the UK. Up to 2,300 species rely on it, including the purple hairstreak butterfly (*Quercusia quercus*) – whose larvae feed exclusively on oak – the oak bark beetle, and hundreds of other insects. By hosting a wealth of invertebrate species, the oak is therefore a vital food source for birds such as chaffinches and wood warblers. Furthermore, its acorns provide vital sustenance for mammals such as wild boar and squirrels.

Oak buds.

It's a fairly well-known saying that 'tall oaks from little acorns grow', but it can take up to fifty years for an oak to reach the age at which it can produce these fruits. The majority of the 90,000 acorns a mature oak might drop in autumn will get eaten, but some of those that have been secreted away by squirrels and jays will be forgotten, and become the great oaks of the future.

Birch

Nearly everyone recognises the slender and graceful silver birch (*Betula pendula*) due to its unique white bark that peels off in strips, as well the black eyes that stare out of it, with groupings of the tree evoking enchanting Scandinavian forests. Less known is the downy birch (*Betula pubescens*), which has a bark that is grey-brown and non-papery.

The silver birch is adorned with triangular leaves that turn gold in autumn. The downy birch's leaves are more rounded and hang from down-covered stalks (hence the name). The two tree species hybridise freely with one another.

Where birch trees grow, fungi such as chanterelles, woolly milk caps and ruby red fly agarics grow beside them – you can see these in autumn. The birch's roots spread across a vast area underground, enabling it to get hold of difficult-to-access nutrients. It absorbs these and passes some to its neighbouring fungi, releasing the rest when its leaves fall to the ground. As these break down during winter, the quality of the soil is improved, and thus the tree is of great benefit to its environment.

In woodlands mostly populated by birch trees, delicate flowers such as wood anemones, bluebells and violets can grow, thanks to the sunlight that reaches the woodland floor through the trees' light, open canopy.

Silver birch bark.

In addition, over 300 species of insects rely on birch trees. Ladybirds eat the aphids and the birds eat moth caterpillars from the leaves, as well as seeds from the catkins. Woodpeckers also favour this tree, nesting within holes in its trunk.

In folklore, birch trees are associated with witches and the supernatural. The classic witch's broomstick is said to be made from bundles of birch branches tied to a hazel handle. In contrast, birch sticks were used to drive away malevolent spirits and were placed above doorways to keep them out. However, there are some positive connections too: the trunk of a birch tree was the maypole around which people across Western Europe danced on 1 May, and in Wales, wreaths made from birch branches were given as symbols of love.

For over 200,000 years, birch bark has been used to make a strong adhesive; Neanderthals glued axe heads onto handles with it. In recent times, birch wood has been transformed into furniture, farming equipment, carts, utensils, and many other useful items. Finally, the betulic acid in the bark may end up being used to fight cancer (research is ongoing).

Hazel

At the very beginning of the year, an early show of colour comes from the handsome golden catkins that dangle from the hazel tree. Also known as lambs' tails, these long thin strands are the male flowers that release millions of pollen grains onto the breeze. You will see them hanging, singly or in pairs, along the branches. The female parts are much more discrete, being tiny fuchsia-coloured flowers that peek out of light green buds on the twig. They are fertilised when they catch the airborne pollen from the male catkins.

Hazel catkins (male) and pink flowers (female).

Although both parts appear on the same tree, fertilisation only occurs across separate trees – the tree cannot self-fertilise. In autumn, fertilised female flowers develop into clusters of hazelnuts. The buds at the end of the twigs, that do not have flowers, will grow into additional branches and leaves.

You will often find distinct groups of hazel trees gathered together in what is called a copse. If the trees have multiple stems growing from a stool that has been cut at ground level, you will know that they have been coppiced. This is a technique carried out by a woodland worker called a coppicer, who cuts back the trees to encourage the new growth. The new stems can be used for hurdles, fencing and decoration, as well as for furniture.

If you notice lots of empty hazelnut shells on the woodland floor surrounding the trees, then you can be quite confident that you have found hazels.

Alder

The alder is a taller, more imposing tree than the hazel. It prefers damp areas and will grow next to streams. Because the wood can tolerate stints of being both wet and dry, it is the ideal material for canal locks.

The alder's catkins are sturdier and knobblier than the hazel's. They open early in the year, in February and March, and will initially appear greener, then more orange or pink than the hazel catkins. They hang in groups at the ends of the branches, with little red-tipped flowers – the female part – appearing above them. The female flowers of the tree come out at a different time to its male catkins, so that they are fertilised by pollen from other alder trees rather than their own. The flowers then turn into modest-sized cones that disperse seeds; seeds which can float and travel downstream.

The tree holds onto its dark green rounded leaves well into November, and old alders have grey fissured bark similar to that of old oaks. In winter, birds such as siskins and redpolls will eat the seeds that they prize out of the cones.

Elder

The elder tree is usually skinny and spindly, with numerous stalks and arching branches of a creamy brown or grey colour. The corky bark is dotted with warts and crisscrossed with deep ridges. The buds are miniature ragged purple pineapples that expand over winter, once the rest of last year's leaves have fallen.

This tree can frequently be found on the edge of woodlands, since it quickly colonises disturbed ground.

In the past, the tree's soft pith was scooped out of the middle of its brittle twigs to make pipes and peashooters – hence its other name of 'pipe-tree' or 'bore-tree'.

Cherry

Cherry buds are similar to oak buds; however, the cherry's bark, with its reddish-purple sheen and morse-code-style dot-and-dash horizontal markings, distinguish it from the oak. Extra bud clusters on the sides of the branches give us abundant blossom in spring. The single buds are those from which the leaves will grow.

Pussy willow

Also known as goat willow or sallow, pussy willow is easy to identify in late winter, when the fluffy grey male catkins appear, reminiscent of the paws of kittens or bunnies. As with the ash, these trees are either male or female (dioecious), while most other trees (such as the birch and oak) are both at the same time (monoecious). The catkins of the female trees are spiky and green.

The fluffy male catkins of pussy willow.

Beech

Beech buds are similar to oak buds, but longer and pointier, and do not appear in clusters.

While many trees bear the eye-shaped scars of fallen branches on their trunks, these are especially noticeable on the smooth grey bark of the beech tree.

It prefers to grow in chalk or light sandy soil, using its deep roots to access moisture. When the trees are resplendent with luminous green leaves in summer, little light will reach the woodland floor, and therefore few plants can grow beneath them.

In winter, animals such as badgers, deer and mice, and birds, including chaffinches and bramblings, will feast on the fallen beech nuts, known as beech mast.

Horse chestnut

The buds of the horse chestnut tree stand out as they are exceptionally large. Dark red and very sticky (an excellent defence mechanism), they are usually covered in minute flies that have met their fate.

On the twigs you can find scars that indicate where the previous buds and leaves were: a collection of lines around the twig show where the buds were; semi-circular scars with dots (horseshoe in shape – hence the name) are where the leaves were. The dots are where the veins ran from the twig into the leaf.

Sticky horse chestnut buds.

Berries

In the cases where the seeds of a fruit are rather substantial – such as in hawthorn berries – birds tend to eat the fleshy part of the fruit but spit the seed out. These seeds therefore do not travel far from the parent plant, and so the hedgerow thickens with these tree species. Blackberries, on the other hand, are consumed seeds and all by both birds and mammals, and so the seeds of the bramble plant can travel greater distances across the woodland. This means that, due to the dispersal of the seeds in faeces, brambles can be found nearly everywhere in the woodland. In winter, the red holly berries are one of the few brilliant colours, and on frosty days it will seem as if they are dusted with icing sugar.

Ivy

As you walk around the woodland observing the trees, you will notice that many tree trunks are swaddled in ivy. The leaves of young ivy plants will bear the classic ivy shape, while those of the mature plants that have thrived will be glossy and oval shaped. This vital plant provides a sanctuary for countless insects that overwinter in the woodlands, and is a shelter and home for birds.

On frosty days in late winter, the ivy's leaves glitter in the sunshine with vibrant lime green and purple veins. Its pink-purple-green-blue berries will be encrusted with ice, resembling a dessert sprinkled with crunchy sugar pieces. Birds such as mistle thrushes adore them.

Holly

Holly leaves are shiny and tough in texture, which keeps moisture in. This is why this tree, which can grow up to 25 metres in height, is able to hold onto its leaves throughout autumn and winter. This makes the holly an evergreen broadleaved tree. The spiked shape of the leaves not only remind us of Christmas festivities, but they ward off browsing animals, such as deer. Holly branches, in the times before Christianity, were brought indoors during the darkest seasons to ward off evil spirits.

The dense cover provided by the holly tree gives year-round shelter to small mammals such as hedgehogs and provides safe nesting sites for birds in spring. Both partake in its berries, which only grow on the female holly tree. This is another favourite food of the mistle thrush.

The first flowers

In winter, primroses, daffodils and snowdrops start to appear, with other flowers following soon after.

Snowdrops

These petite porcelain flowers hang their heads shyly from long emerald-green stems. Gathering in groups, they appear in patches here and there, or spread across woodland floors, sometimes poking out from blankets of snow. Their scientific name of *Galanthus nivalis* comes from the Greek, '*Galanthus*' meaning 'milk-flower', with '*nivalis*' meaning 'snow-white' or 'growing near snow'. Due to climate change, they appear earlier and earlier each year. Coming originally from continental Europe, they naturalised in Britain, from gardens to woodlands, in the sixteenth century.

Snowdrops.

Primrose

This cheery bloom is connected to the brimstone butterfly – the first butterfly of the year to flit along the woodland edges – heralding spring. The butterfly is the same bright yellow as the classic primrose, which used to be the first flower of the year, leading to its name, 'prima rosa' (first rose). However, the introduced snowdrop has now beaten the primrose to it.

The primrose's squat cluster of flowers is a nectar source for both the brimstone and the small tortoiseshell butterfly. The rare Duke of Burgundy butterfly favours this plant, laying its precious eggs on the furry underside of the long, green, crinkly leaves. Other early-flying insects such as bees benefit from the presence of the primrose in the woodland.

There are two types of primrose. The 'thrum-eyed' one has a yellow pom-pom in its centre with a stamen and a cluster of anthers above it, and the 'pin-eyed' one has a green circle within, with a stigma. Insects travel between the two, providing the necessary pollination service in return for sustenance.

Despite appearances, each primrose flower has only one petal. This petal is indented in five places along its top edge, which gives the suggestion of five petals. So look closely next time you come across a primrose plant: you'll see that the five 'parts' are actually joined together as one.

Primrose flowers were once infused in water as a tea taken for hysteria, and for its sedative properties. The leaves were used in salads.

If left undisturbed, primrose plants will bloom from February to May for decades.

Primrose.

Winter aconites, crocuses and daffodils

At the same time as you find snowdrops in the gaps between the trees and in open parts of the woodland or along its edges, you may come across colourful winter aconites and crocuses in gorgeous shades of lavender, deep purple and yellow. Standing above these will be daffodils, welcomed by all as a sign of the forthcoming spring, their trumpet faces bringing a smile to many of us on a cold and overcast day.

Lesser celandines

Lesser celandines begin to bloom in late winter, around 21 February, the date on which the pioneering parson-naturalist Gilbert White observed them appearing in Selborne in 1795. The naturalists who followed in his footsteps have noted a similar result and so, unknown to a lot of modern people, this date became known as Celandine Day. Interestingly, lesser celandines were the poet William Wordsworth's favourite flower – it wasn't the daffodil, as you would expect!

These golden and star-shaped waxy flowers, with eight to twelve petals, have been called 'spring messengers', and represent 'joys to come'. 'Celandine' comes from the Greek word '*chelidon*', which means 'swallow'; in the same way as these birds, they herald the start of spring. What's more, their dark green and glossy heart-shaped leaves bring joy to those who stumble across this early-flowering wildflower.

Growing in damp, shady patches of the woodland – gleaming in the gloom – lesser celandines will hang around until May.

Lesser celandine.

Birds

On cold days, birds will fluff up their feathers, creating an insulating layer of air between their skin and the surrounding atmosphere. This preserves their body heat. On sunny winter days, the birds make the most of the extra warmth from the sun to forage for remaining berries and seeds.

Amongst the glittering cobwebs, goldfinches swarm the teasels and hang daintily from the skinny stalks which hardly bend under their weight. Blackbirds gobble up the leftover sloes from the otherwise naked blackthorn (see the photo on page 60), and redwings plunder the rowan trees for orange berries.

Whatever the weather, robins will cheer you with their fluty song, promising that others will join them in a few months for the spring concert.

If your woodland borders a meadow or field, you might even hear a skylark sing – appearing as a mere speck in the sky – claiming its territory. In the leafless trees you can locate last year's birds' nests. Some of these may get reused when spring arrives.

Starlings

From autumn onwards, these spangled, metallic-hued birds return from northern Europe to join our resident starlings.

By the middle of winter, the starling population will have swelled to 500,000 individuals in some places, filling the trees and skies with the excited whistles, clicks and calls that they have stolen from other birds.

In the evenings they will gather in high-flying flocks, converging with others to create pulsating, rippling patterns. This is called a murmuration. After this impressive display, they will return to the trees to roost for the night, chattering noisily as they do.

Starling.

THE SECRET LIFE OF A WOODLAND HABITAT

Corvids

Also spending time in groups are the corvids. During the day, you may see up to 30 magpies being sociable in a tree, 'chack-chacking' away. When conditions improve and the mating season begins, they will split off into pairs. These are the easiest corvids to recognise (apart from the jay), being black and white and sporting long iridescent tails.

The jackdaw has a short beak, grey hood and pale eyes. Its call is a sharp 'jac', just like its name. The rook is bigger and glossy black, with a long and pointed pale grey beak. Its call is a loud 'kaah', and in winter it will return to its tree-top rookery to rebuild a hefty nest next to its neighbours. The carrion crow is completely black and slightly bigger than the rook, and possesses a powerful beak. Its call is a hoarse, croaky 'craah', although you might hear it making a gurgling sound or other strange noises too.

Jackdaws, rooks and crows will fly in flocks in the evening, cawing away, travelling from wherever they have been foraging during the day to go back to their woodland roost. On misty or overcast days, it is incredibly atmospheric to witness the birds filling up the sky with their ominous shapes and sounds.

They all feed on small mammals, insects, carrion and fruit, as well as the eggs and young of other birds during the warmer seasons.

Great spotted woodpecker.

Woodpeckers

The two common woodpeckers in the UK are the great spotted woodpecker and the green woodpecker (see photo on the back cover). The first is a striking black and white bird, roughly the size of a blackbird, with a red rump. In addition, the male has a red patch on the back of its head. The green woodpecker is larger and vivid green, with a yellow rump, black moustache (that is filled with red in the male) and a red patch on its head.

You will need both sharp eyes and luck to catch sight of these shy birds. Plus, if they realise that they are being watched, they will frequently move round to the other side of the tree, or fly away! The great spotted woodpecker is rarely seen on the ground, instead choosing to stay high in the canopy in its search for insects, nuts, berries and seeds, moving from tree to tree with a deeply undulating flight. However, you might catch a glimpse of the green woodpecker flying low between patches of woodland after feasting on ants. The latter will laugh or 'yaffle' when on the wing.

Both woodpeckers have feet consisting of two forward-facing claws and two backward-facing ones, which gives them the ability to hold on at perilous angles while foraging for food, sounding their drumming calls and making their nesting holes in tree trunks. Another useful feature is their long tongue (around 10cm) which is curled around their skull when not being used to probe deep into bark or soil to hoover up food.

Long-tailed tits

It is the high-pitched plaintive 'see' calls of the long-tailed tits that will first grab your attention. Then you will discern these attractive black, white and pink lollipops darting between the branches of bushes, searching for minute insects to eat. At this time of year, they must spend 90% of the day feeding in order to survive the long winter nights. They travel around in a flock of up to thirty individuals during the day, then huddle together in small roosts at night.

Male sparrowhawk.

Kestrels and sparrowhawks

On a winter's day, you might be lucky enough to encounter a kestrel or sparrowhawk hunting for a meal. The former will hover high in the sky in open areas or perch on a branch before swooping down on an unsuspecting rodent; the latter will stalk groups of birds such as finches through the woodland, darting in to pick off the vulnerable when the opportunity presents itself.

When first glimpsing a male sparrowhawk in the trees, you might believe that you are observing a wood pigeon. But when you look again, you'll notice the orange under his chin and his sinister black and orange eye. As well as small birds, the sparrowhawk will take pigeons when it can, plucking the feathers from its victim before tucking in.

Goldfinch

Right now you have a good chance of spying flocks of goldfinches clinging onto the stems of dried plants, such as thistles and teasels, extracting the seeds using their long slim beaks. The goldfinch is a very eye-catching bird, with a red face, white cheek, black cap, and black and yellow wings. The male and female are almost identical.

Goldcrest

This dainty bird (the smallest in the UK) is a light greenish-brown, with barring on its wings and a striking head-stripe that is yellow, orange and black on the male and yellow and black on the female. Keep an eye out for it flitting amongst the ivy, often hanging upside down or hovering to feed on flies and spiders from the undersides of the leaves. While the goldcrest regularly visits deciduous woodlands, it is particularly prevalent in conifer woodlands. The majority of the goldcrests you observe are part of our resident population; however, some do come over from Northern Europe to spend winter in the UK. They will sometimes join flocks of tits as they move through the woodland.

Wren

This brown individual with its flicking pointed-up tail is the second-smallest bird in the UK after the goldcrest. It is therefore likely that you will hear it rather than see it. The wren tends to flit between low branches, or stay deep within dense vegetation, hopping along the ground to grab insects from the moss and undergrowth. The wren's song is surprisingly loud considering its size: a fast warbling, usually with a trill at the end. With less foliage around, you might glimpse its shape in the shadows, or witness the rare moment when it reveals itself for a second or two before disappearing once again.

Wren.

Chaffinch

The male chaffinch has a pinkish breast, a grey cap on his head, two sizable white bars across his wings, and white outer tail feathers. The female has the white outer tail feathers and wing-bars, but is otherwise browner and better camouflaged against tree branches. This is a bird of bountiful songs, so listen out for the call that is easier to recognise: a loud 'tink' or 'pink'.

Over winter, migrant chaffinches that have come from Norway and Sweden will travel round together in mainly single-sex groups.

The chaffinch's chunky beak, in a shape common to all the finches, is ideal for prizing seeds from various plants as well as from beech mast. They also eat insects.

Siskin

This bird is the size of a blue tit and similar in colour to the greenfinch, being yellowish-green. It can be told apart from the latter by its yellow and black wing-bars, as well as by the black cap on the males. It feeds on the seeds from pine, alder and birch trees.

Tawny owl

The tawny owl hunts at night in the woodland, often perching in a tree and dropping down onto its prey, which mainly consists of small mammals and birds, but sometimes worms and insects too. This is when they can be heard calling to one another: one sounding a haunting 'hoohoo-oo-ooo' and the other a harsh 'kewick'. The tawny owl nests within holes in trees, and spends the day there or on a branch close to the tree's trunk. It is roughly the size of a wood pigeon and is mottled with various shades of brown and cream.

Tawny owl.

Song thrush

It is hard to ignore this bird's song. Singing high up in a tall tree, such as a larch, the song thrush repeats a phrase 2–4 times before moving onto the next phrase. It's an odd song, in a tone that almost doesn't sound bird-like, but it is complex and intriguing, and increasingly enjoyable the longer you listen to it. Smaller than a blackbird, the song thrush has a brown back and a creamy breast dotted with brown spots.

Mistle thrush

With its speckled breast, this mistletoe-lover is similarly patterned to the song thrush, but is larger in size and greyer in colour. The tone of its melodious music is comparable to the song thrush's and blackbird's; however the delivery of its song is slower and the whistling phrases, which are repeated 3–6 times, are less varied than those of the song thrush.

   The mistle thrush has been called a 'storm-cock' as, unlike a lot of other bird species, it will sing even as winds rise and storm clouds gather.

Nuthatch

Look up the side of a tall tree. You might detect a shape climbing with short hops up and down the trunk – a nuthatch. This half grey-blue, half orangey-yellow bird with a black stripe across its eye will nest in a tree hole, the entrance of which is edged with mud until only the nuthatch can fit through it – thus protecting the bird's young from predators. Although it will feed on the ground at times, this secretive bird will normally stay on the tree, wedging nuts into the cracks of the bark so that it can hammer away at them until it gets to the goodness inside. It also eats insects. Listen out for its call ('tuwit tuwit') and its song ('quee-quee-quee') to help you ascertain its whereabouts.

Nuthatch.

Treecreeper

Even more aloof than the nuthatch, the treecreeper can be difficult to detect and then watch for longer than a few seconds. Its habit is to spiral up and round a tree trunk as it browses for food. It will pick out insects and spiders from between the fissures of the bark with its long downward-curving beak, its mottled back feathers in various shades of brown providing excellent camouflage against the bark. In winter it will shelter behind loose bark and in crevices, and in spring build nests in these places (see the photo on page 11). Its call is a high-pitched 'tsee tsse' and its song is a 'see see see, sissi-see' that speeds up towards the end.

Blackbird

The black male and brown female are busy scuttling in the undergrowth, turning over dead leaves beneath trees and bushes in their search for worms, snails, millipedes and insects. They make such a noise doing so that you will suspect a human moving around in there. They are both rather shy at this time of year, and vocally quiet too. Yet, once disturbed by your presence, they will fly away sounding their alarm call.

By the end of the season, however, the male will start to sing. As well as enjoying his delightful music, you can be assured that spring is on its way!

Insects

On milder days, some insects stir themselves from their torpor to seek the nectar of early-flowering plants, becoming an extra food source themselves for birds.

In the same conditions, you can spy bees venturing out for early flowers such as snowdrops, primroses and dandelions.

Right now, queen tree wasps are hibernating under the bark. They will form new colonies in spring.

Mammals

Mice, voles, shrews, rats and moles

Chestnut-brown bank voles live in shallow burrows within woodlands and adjoining hedgerows. Blackberries and hazelnuts are their favourite food, but they will eat other fruit, nuts and insects. Active year-round, bank voles do not hibernate, and can give birth to up to five young, up to four times a year. They live for 1.5 years on average. They are prey to kestrels, owls and weasels. Voles have wider faces, smaller ears and shorter tails than mice.

Wood mice are one of the most common woodland rodents in the UK. They have golden-brown fur and pale undersides, and live in underground burrows and old birds' nests. They do not hibernate, and females can have up to six litters a year, each containing as many as eight young. If food is abundant, they can even breed during winter. Tawny owls are especially dependent on wood mice to survive, as they form the majority of their diet.

Hazel dormice are rarer rodents – found in only a few places in the UK – and are a protected species. They hibernate from November to March in nests made out of grass and leaves. In spring and summer, they will climb up trees at night to find hazelnuts, berries and insects to eat.

There are three species of shrew in the UK: water shrews, common shrews and pygmy shrews. All three have pointier noses than mice, and tiny eyes. Water shrews (which live in wetland habitats) are the largest, being up to 9.5cm in length, while common shrews are up to 8cm, and pygmy shrews can be as little as 4cm. Living for up to two years, common and pygmy shrews snuffle in the undergrowth eating insects and earthworms. In

Bank vole.

order to survive, common shrews need to eat 80–90% of their body weight every day! All three shrews are active throughout the year, and are protected under the Wildlife and Countryside Act, 1981.

Brown rats, who came to the UK in the 1700s as stowaways on ships, are now widespread here. They live in burrows as part of loose colonies, and are larger than all the mice species, at up to 27cm in length. Brown rats will eat almost anything and can breed throughout the year, which has led to their success. The females become sexually mature at just three months old and can give birth to up to twelve young, five times a year.

Moles are widespread in the UK and active throughout the year; however, since they spend the majority of their lives underground, they are rarely seen by human eyes. They dig tunnels through the earth in their search for their favourite food – earthworms – although they will eat grubs on their way. As a result of their hard work, the soil is aerated and thus healthier, allowing plants to grow and water to drain through. They have black, velvety fur, two pink spade-like front paws, tiny eyes and a long pink nose.

Stoat.

Weasels and stoats

Weasels and stoats are widespread and active year-round. Related to otters, they have long slender bodies and short legs. Weasels move close to the ground with a running gait and straight back, whereas stoats bound along, arching their backs as they do so.

Weasels are up to 22cm in length, with a tail of up to 5cm, and they live for around two years. They are our smallest carnivore and can hunt day or night, preying on mice, voles and birds. They give birth once or twice a year, with three to six kits per litter. Their backs are russet-brown, while their bellies and throats are white.

Stoats are bigger than weasels at up to 32cm in length and can live for up to five years. They hunt the same prey as weasels, with the addition of more sizable animals, such as adult rabbits. They kill by delivering a lethal bite to the base of their victim's skull. They have one litter per year, consisting of six to twelve kits. Their backs are orangey-brown; their throats and bellies are creamy white. Their tails have black tips and are longer than weasels' tails, at up to 14cm. In regions where it is very cold, stoats' coats can become paler and even white, so that they can successfully hunt in the snow.

Rabbits and hares

These long-eared mammals can be seen across the UK, living on the edges of woodland: the former in underground warrens; the latter in shallow depressions on adjoining fields. Rabbits were introduced by the Normans from Spain in the twelfth century, as a source of food and fur, while it is believed that hares were

Red squirrel.

introduced by the Romans, although it may have been earlier. Both are active year-round, grazing on vegetation and the bark of young bushes and trees. They are preyed upon by foxes, stoats and buzzards. Female rabbits produce one litter of up to seven babies every month of their breeding season, and female hares produce up to four litters of a maximum four leverets per year. The easiest way to tell the two apart is by the ears: hares have longer ears, with black tips. They have longer legs and are larger in size compared to rabbits.

Squirrels

UK woodlands are predominantly populated by grey squirrels, which were introduced from North America in the nineteenth century as a fashionable addition to country estates. Since then, they have moved into our woodlands and across the UK. Sadly, since grey squirrels out-compete red squirrels for food and territory, and carry a virus that kills red squirrels, the number of red squirrels has declined significantly. So much so that they are now classed as an endangered species. However, there are areas in which the native red squirrels still live, including Scotland, Wales, Norfolk, the Isle of Wight and the Lake District. Black variants of the grey squirrel exist too – these can be found in Bedfordshire, Hertfordshire and Cambridgeshire.

In winter, grey squirrels' fur is silvery grey, with a brown tinge that runs along the middle of their backs. Their underparts are white, their bushy tails are grey, and their ears do not have tufts. Red squirrels do have tufts on their ears and their coats are reddish with white underparts.

Hazelnut shells on a woodland floor.

At this time of year, squirrels do not hibernate. Instead, they build a thick drey to nestle within on particularly cold days. The drey is a football-sized nest made of twigs and lined with feathers, moss, bark and dry grass, positioned high up in a tree. They will tuck into the nuts that they gathered in autumn: hazelnuts, beech mast and acorns. They will also eat fungi, tree bark and buds. Under their preferred tree, the woodland floor will be littered with discarded nut shells.

Later in the season, squirrels begin courting – the males chasing the females across the ground, through the trees, or around the trunks. The impregnated females will give birth six weeks later, in March or April, to an average litter of three babies (it can be up to nine). The males do not help with the rearing of the young.

Deer

In the UK, there six types of deer living in the wild: roe, Scottish red, Reeves' muntjac, fallow, sika and Chinese water. Of those, only the roe and red are truly indigenous, with the rest being introduced to the UK at some point in the distant or recent past. The Normans introduced the fallow deer, while the muntjac, sika and Chinese water deer arrived on our shores during the nineteenth and twentieth centuries.

Roe deer are medium-sized, at less than a metre tall. They are abundant across the UK and are mostly noticeable at the edges of woodlands. In winter, their coats are grey, brown or even black – but this changes again in summer. They have a distinctive white rump, but no discernible tail. Their large noses, eyes and mouths, combined with huge ears, makes them very attractive, and the eponymous character in the original *Bambi* book by Felix Salten was based on this deer. The males (bucks) have modest, heavily-textured antlers with three points. They live for ten years on average. During winter, the generally solitary deer form small groups.

Red deer are taller than roe deer, standing at up to 1.22 metres for the females (hinds) and 1.37 metres for the males (stags) at the shoulder. They are found in immense numbers in Scotland, which is why they are also known as 'Scottish red deer', although they are distributed across parts of England as well. At this time of year, they have a brown winter coat. Their rumps are pale and they have short tails. The size of their heads is considerable and their brown eyes are widely spaced. The males are particularly recognisable, with their impressive and highly-branched antlers. They live for eighteen years on average.

Muntjac deer are diminutive deer, at about half a metre in height. Their coats are dull grey in winter, but a russet brown for the rest of the year. With rumps higher than their shoulders, they have a hunched appearance and a flat, white tail. The males (bucks) sport vertical black lines on their faces and pale cheeks. Their antlers are small, inward curving, and non-branching. The females (does) have a dark patch on the top of their heads. There is something about the facial expression of these deer, combined with their colouring, that is reminiscent

Muntjac.

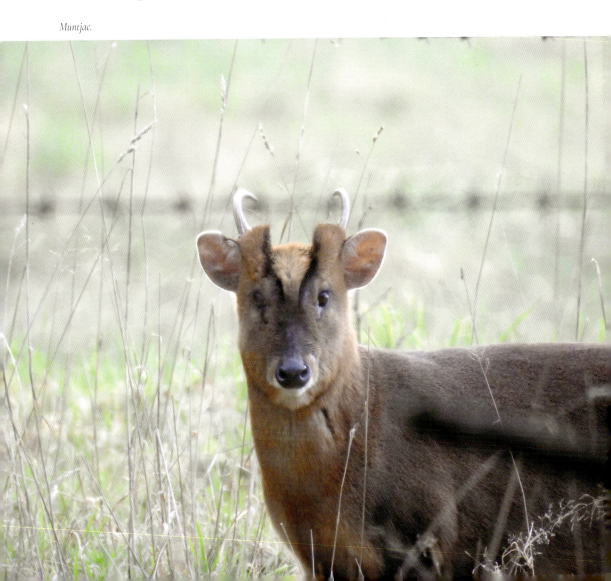

of a teddy bear. Muntjac were introduced from China to Woburn Park in Bedfordshire in the early twentieth century. Since then, they have spread across the south and central regions of the UK. They live up to eighteen years on average.

Fallow deer are medium to large deer, at nearly a metre in height. There are four main variations in the colouring of their coats, but the most common is tan with white patches across the back and sides (although this coat fades to grey in winter), with a white rump bearing a horseshoe-shaped border. Their long tails often have a vertical black line on them, and the horseshoe shape on their rump is frequently outlined with black too. Fallow deer have impressive, palmate antlers that can be up to 0.7 metres in length. Introduced from the eastern Mediterranean in the eleventh century, they are now widespread across England and Wales. They live up to sixteen years on average.

A deer's diet consists of tree shoots, bark, woody plants, fruit, leaves and grass.

Hedgehogs

Beneath dense vegetation and hedgerows, live round, spiky hedgehogs. Each hedgehog has 5,000 to 7,000 inch-long spikes made of keratin (like our fingernails and hair) covering their backs and sides. The rest of their body is covered with a coarse, grey-brown fur.

During winter, hedgehogs are curled up in their nests, hibernating.

Badgers

The largest remaining native predator in the UK since wolves, bears and wild boar were persecuted and hunted to extinction, the badger is the enigmatic king of the woodland. The instantly-recognisable black, white and grey member of the Mustelid family (that includes otters and pine martens) lives as part of a mixed-sex group in a sprawling underground den called a sett. The sett is formed of multiple entrances and chambers, and is reused and passed down the generations.

Cubs are born in January and February, having been conceived between February and May of the previous year. After spending their first two months of life safely below ground, the cubs will begin to emerge between March and April.

Foxes

Alongside the badger, the fox is at the top of the woodland food chain, with a varied diet consisting of earthworms, insects, fruit, birds and small to medium mammals. Foxes and badgers do sometimes compete for food; however, there are also cases of them sharing badger setts. As with many mammals, foxes tend to forage at dawn and dusk. Even if you do not encounter any foxes while walking through a woodland, certain signs – such as scat in prominent positions and on footpaths – indicate their presence.

Winter is a very important time for foxes, as it is when they breed. To facilitate this, they are very vocal at night-time, screeching and barking to attract mates and warn rivals. Usually, only one vixen per social group (containing three to four adults) breeds – but it can be up to three.

Later in the season, vixens will create several potential breeding earths by digging holes at the edges of the woodland, in preparation for giving birth in spring.

Bats

Over a quarter of our mammal species are bats, and they all eat insects. Each foraging bat will catch thousands of insects per night.

Of the eighteen species of bat in the UK, those that are woodland specialists – meaning those that prefer to roost and forage in this environment – include noctules, Bechstein's (one of our rarest bats), barbastelles (also

Fox.

rare), brown long-eared bats and pipistrelles. Noctules live in small to medium-sized woodlands, in tree holes that have been created by woodpeckers or rot, while Bechstein's bats will live in ash and oak trees in extensive wet woodlands with streams. Barbastelles prefer old or ancient woodlands and roost within splits in trees or behind loose bark. Brown long-eared bats, unlike the others, can live in roosts closer to the ground, surrounded by vegetation, and eat insects from bark and leaves. Pipistrelles (both the common and soprano species) reside in woodlands year-round and are amongst the most common bat species in the UK.

Two other bats which forage in woodlands (although they rarely roost in them) are the lesser and greater horseshoe bats, which catch midges and moths as they manoeuvre easily between the trees.

The noctule is the largest UK bat, with a head and body length of 6.5–8cm and a wingspan of 35cm; the common pipistrelle meanwhile is the smallest with a head and body length of 4cm and a wingspan of 20cm.

Bats spend the cold winter months in hibernation, surviving on the fat reserves that they built up in autumn. However, if there are particularly mild nights, some may leave the roost to find water and feast on the insects that have also woken up.

CHAPTER 2

Spring

Spring is full of shining things:
Bees that buzz and birds that sing;
The blackthorn bursts and blooms and glows
– All life is here, as nature knows.

Chloé Valerie Harmsworth

Introduction

If spring could be defined by just one word, it would be excitement. Or perhaps potential. The days lengthen and become brighter, with the intense light shining on little sparks of life: the budding trees bursting into bloom; the birds becoming increasingly numerous and vocal; the insects buzzing and flitting everywhere. There is more happening in the woodland than can be seen in one outing, and so every walk is rewarded with a bounty of natural delights. It is this, as well as the milder days and regular sunshine – that lights up the blossom and emerging flowers – that makes it many people's favourite season.

Following on from your learning of trees during the winter, you can now revisit the trees to find out what they are doing in spring. Studying the new leaves, catkins and flowers will help to confirm your identification of them.

Robin in blossom.

Make the most of the birds you can see at the beginning of spring as, by summer, they will be enclosed in the canopy of the fully-leaved trees. Before this happens, enjoy their songs, admire their many-coloured feathers and watch as they eagerly build their nests ready for egg laying.

The insects are one of the other stars of this season, with a gorgeous array of butterflies appearing, seduced by the sunshine, blossom and colourful wildflowers, and bringing much delight to the woodland wanderer.

Trees, bushes and plants

Elder
One of the first trees to burst into leaf is the elder tree. Bright lime-green leaves unfurl from amethyst buds. Although the leaves and wood of the elder emit an unpleasant smell, it won't be long until this is overshadowed by the deliciously floral scent of the frothy clumps of creamy flowers that appear later in spring. These elderflowers can be used to make elderflower wine or champagne.

In the past the soft pith was scooped from the middle of the brittle twigs to make pipes and peashooters, hence its other name of 'pipe-tree' or 'bore-tree'.

Wild cherry
The wild cherry tree will be one of the first trees that you'll find covered in blossom. As well as providing a wonderful sight for our eyes, the delicate white flowers that dangle on stalks in clusters are an important early source of nectar and pollen for bees and other insects. After pollination, they will transform into cherries,

Grey squirrel eating cherries.

initially green and then turning deep-red. At this time of year, you might spy a cheeky squirrel hanging from its tail, eating the unripe cherries!

The ripe cherries are consumed by numerous birds, including the fruit-loving blackbird, and mammals such as badgers, dormice and wood mice. The leaves are oval-shaped, pointed and toothed all around the edges. The leaves are the main food plant for the caterpillars of multiple moth species, such as the brimstone moth.

Hawthorn

The hawthorn is also one of the first trees to reveal its leaves in spring: they are modest in size, with toothed lobes. By mid-May, this tree (which often appears as part of a hedgerow) will be covered in heavily-scented pale-pink or white five-petalled flowers in flat clusters. It is the timing of this blossom that gives the tree its other name of 'May-tree'. These flowers are beloved by bees and eaten by dormice.

It is the ideal tree for nesting birds as its thorny structure protects their young from predators, and the dense foliage in late spring and summer hides them from prying eyes. Once pollinated, the flowers turn into diminutive red berries called haws. In pagan symbolism, the hawthorn was associated with fertility.

Blackthorn

In early spring, the spiky blackthorn shrubs will turn snowy white with flowers that appear on short stalks singularly or in pairs. This is where you can observe the first bees and butterflies, such as the peacock butterfly (see the photo on page 62), finding their first sustenance of the year. Small, pointed and toothed leaves appear after this. The pollinated flowers will turn into blue-black marbles, called sloes, by late summer.

This is another excellent tree for nesting birds, since it provides both shelter and a buffet of insects to feed their young with. In mythology, the blackthorn has been associated with witchcraft – with witches' wands apparently being made from its wood.

Ash

In spring, the black hooves of the ash tree split open, and from them emerge a fountain of purple flowers. These are pollinated by the wind and develop into winged fruit, called keys, in late summer and autumn. In spring, last year's keys are dropped, to be eaten and dispersed by birds and animals, although some are still being eaten straight off the tree by goldfinches and other birds (see the photo on page 19).

Once the leaves appear, you will notice that they are formed of 3–6 opposite pairs of oval leaflets with a single leaflet at the end. This is somewhat similar to rowan leaves, although the edges of those are serrated.

English oak

Most people won't even realise that this tree has catkins in April and May, as they are subtler than those on other trees. Yellow and delicate, the long male catkins hang in curtains from the ends of the twigs, amongst the young leaves. The female flowers are even harder to see, being miniature red protrusions with fine filaments that catch the wind-blown pollen – once pollinated, they will become acorns in time for autumn. The deeply-lobed leaves grow in bunches and are around 10cm in length once fully grown, with smooth edges.

Silver birch

Hanging at the end of the twigs, in groups of two or four, the male catkins of the silver birch are yellowy-brown and shorter than hazel catkins. The female catkins are even shorter and bright green, until they thicken and turn dark crimson following pollination. From these, seeds will be released onto autumn winds, on miniscule wings that help them travel to new destinations.

The leaves are small and triangular, with a toothed edge.

Oak tree leafing, with catkins.

Pussy (goat) willow

The infinitely strokable male catkins now turn yellow with ripe pollen, attracting the bees who transfer the pollen from the catkins of the male trees to the catkins of the female trees as they collect the nectar that both secrete. The yellow stigmas of the female catkins catch the male pollen from the insect's hairs and, once pollinated, turn into a green fruit. These then split open to release woolly seeds to be carried away by the wind in the early summer.

The leaves are oval with fine grey hairs on the underside. The tips of them bend to one side. The foliage is a food plant for many species of moth, as well as the purple emperor butterfly.

Unlike most willow tree species, pussy willow twigs are brittle and therefore not suitable for weaving. Salicin, which is found in the bark of all willow (salix) species, is a compound used in aspirin. It is appropriate then that the bark of willows used to be chewed by people to relieve toothache and headaches.

The word 'willow' is said to be the source of the words 'wicked', 'witch' and 'Wiccan', which indicates its association with witchcraft.

Male pussy willow catkins ripening with pollen.

Beech

In April and May, the male flowers of the beech tree appear on long stalks that hang from the ends of the twigs. The female flowers, on the other hand, grow in pairs and are surrounded by a cup. Following wind pollination, the cup eventually turns into a spiny outer shell containing the nuts known as beech mast.

The lime green leaves are covered in silky hairs when immature; the mature leaves are hairless, oval and pointy, with a wavy edge.

Hornbeam

The hornbeam is another tree that is pollinated by the wind, when the pollen from the male catkins reaches the female flowers. Subsequently, the female flowers change into green, papery winged fruits with three lobes (see the photo on page 73).

Hornbeam leaves are similar to beech leaves, except that they are smaller, more deeply furrowed and have doubly-serrated edges, unlike the beech leaves' smooth edges.

The tree has a pale grey bark, with deep ridges that sometimes spiral round the trunk.

Horse chestnut leaves and flowers.

Horse chestnut

The sticky red buds of the horse chestnut now begin to split open, and from them burst young leaves curling round immature flowers. Over the following weeks, the palmate leaves of 5–7 toothed and pointed leaflets open up and push out sideways away from the centre, reminiscent of helicopter blades.

Now fully revealed, the flowers in the middle rise up into tall pink or white spires by May. Each individual flower in these candlestick clusters is in the form of a long tube, with nectar at the bottom, which can only be reached by insects with long proboscises (which are straw-like mouthparts that suck up the nectar), such as butterflies and certain bees. After pollination the flowers turn into shiny red-brown fruit enclosed in a spiky green shell. These are the hard nuts that we play the game 'conkers' with, which are eaten by deer and other mammals in autumn.

Sweet chestnut

The sweet chestnut belongs to the same family as the oak and beech trees, and has smooth grey-purple bark with vertical fissures. Its glossy, pointed leaves are very large, at 16–28cm in length, with serrated edges.

In spring, thin yellow catkins appear between the sweet chestnut leaves (see the photo on page 72), consisting of mainly male flowers, but with female flowers at the base of them. After the female flowers have been pollinated by insects, they develop into fruit that appear very similar to conkers, although they are smaller and grow in clusters. The cases of these fruit are much spikier than the horse chestnut's, and contain several fruit within each. These can be eaten and enjoyed by us when autumn comes around.

European larch

The long bendy branches of the larch tree are dotted with brown scaly buds in spring. From these emerge raspberry-shaped and raspberry-coloured flowers or clusters of needles that are 2–4cm long. The male parts appear on the underside of the shoots, with the female flower on the tips. The dark pink flowers, known as larch roses, are in fact the immature female cones. They turn green and expand following wind pollination, eventually becoming the recognisable hard brown cones. These will open their scales in autumn to release their winged seeds. Siskins and red squirrels also prise the seeds from the cones to eat. At the same time, the needles will turn orange and then be shed by the tree. In folklore, the larch is supposed to protect against enchantment.

Larch roses and cones.

Spring flowers

Buttercups

As the days lengthen and the temperatures rise, brighter colours appear on the woodland floor. Buttercups (from the same family as lesser celandines) join the yellow brigade, with their petite shiny petals. It was once believed that if cows grazed pastures containing numerous buttercups, the butter created from their milk would be a very pleasing colour. There's also the beloved question, 'Do I like butter?', which can be answered by holding a buttercup under your chin. If your skin glows yellow, then you do indeed like butter!

Cowslips.

Cowslips

Cowslips are so called since they apparently appear wherever there is cow dung, or because they have a scent that is meant to resemble cows' breath. Another theory is that the wrinkled texture of their leaves is reminiscent of a cow's lip.

At first glance, it is a very similar flower to the primrose; however, there are subtle differences. As with the primrose, the cowslip produces both 'pin-head' and 'thrum-eyed' flowers. The leaves are very much alike too, although the cowslip's ones are egg-shaped. The flower section of the plant is similarly divided into five petal-like parts (that are actually just one petal), although they are more petite than primrose flowers and droop from their stalks. Finally, where the primrose flowers grow singly, on the cowslip several blooms are clustered together on each stalk.

An old name given to the cowslip was paralysis-herb, or palsy-wort, as it was believed that the flower could cure these conditions. You will find this plant growing along the edges of the woodland and under the hedgerow in April and May.

Wood anemones

The wood anemone is an indicator of ancient woodland – woods that have been in existence since 1600 or earlier.

Just before the bluebells arrive, the woodland floor will be scattered in March and April with these sweet, six- to seven-petalled white flowers with prominent yellow stamens. The scientific name for the wood anemone is *Anemone nemorosa*, with 'nemorosa' meaning 'well wooded', indicating the flower's habitat. 'Anemone' is a Greek word for 'wind-flower', as they thought the flower only opened when the wing blew.

The usually pure white petals are sometimes tinged with pink. When the evening comes, or the sky is overcast, the flowers will close up to protect themselves from the cold and rain.

The wood anemone's leaves are divided into three toothed leaflets.

Wood anemone.

Wild garlic

If you are lucky, you will live near a woodland where wild garlic grows. Lovers of damp conditions, swathes of garlic plants often appear on sloping banks or by woodland streams. Emitting a strong oniony smell, the plant is a relative of the cultivated garlic we use for cooking, as well as of onions, leeks and shallots.

Wild garlic has broad, pointed leaves set on long stalks. These gave the plant its name, as 'gar' was the Anglo-Saxon term for spear. 'Lic' comes from the word 'leek', and so the plant was described as the 'spear-leek'. Today, it is commonly known as ramsons.

If you want to gather the plant for culinary use, for example to make a wild garlic pesto from the leaves, the best time to do so is before the clusters of six-pointed white flowers, with the three green balls of seeds within each of them, appear. Be careful though not to confuse the plant with the poisonous lily-of-the-valley, which has very similar leaves. The strong garlic scent of the correct plant will guide you.

Bluebells

The bluebell is the most famous springtime flower, tempting thousands of people each year to search for breath-taking views of blue-purple flowers carpeting woodland floors. The fragrant flowers are beloved by brimstone butterflies, who visit them for their delicious nectar.

These delicately drooping bell flowers are a sign of ancient woodland, as they can only bloom if undisturbed. They appear in late spring (April/May) as the sunlight hits the soil, before the canopy closes in summer leaf. It is said that the wetter the preceding winter is, the more vibrant the bluebells will be in spring.

Bluebells.

They are protected by the Wildlife and Countryside Act 1981, making it illegal to remove them. However, despite this protection, they are vulnerable to trampling by over-eager visitors, keen to get stunning photos amongst the purple-blue. If the plants are crushed, they cannot photosynthesise, and therefore cannot make the food they need. This weakens the plants, so they will not bloom as abundantly in the succeeding springs. It can take years for damaged plants to recover and it doesn't take long for swathes of bluebells to be worn and trampled down to mere patches.

The plants are also becoming hybridised with the introduced Spanish bluebell, which has upright stems and flowers with outspread petals.

Bluebell bulbs contain a sticky substance that has had various uses over time, such as starch for collars and ruffs, and adhesive for book binding.

Stitchwort

When the white stitchwort and cow parsley arrive in April and May, you know that it is well and truly spring, and summer will soon arrive.

Stitchwort's scientific name is *Stellaria holostea*. 'Stellaria' denotes the star shape of the flowers. Another name given to the plant is 'satin-flower', due to its shiny white petals – which are split at the top to give the impression of ten petals instead of five. The common name of stitchwort may have come from an early use of the plant to cure stitches or cramps.

Stinging nettle

This plant, well known by humans for its ability to deliver a frustratingly itchy sting when touched, plays a very important role in the woodland. Growing in large patches almost anywhere, it is a vital food source for the caterpillars of many of our beloved butterflies, such as the small tortoiseshell, peacock and red admiral. Reaching a height of up to 1.2 metres in places, and sporting heart-shaped serrated leaves covered in stinging hairs that inject histamine into the skin upon contact, this plant will flower twice a year, in spring and then autumn. These appear as thin catkins of tiny yellow-green to purple flowers.

The plant spreads with the help of its seeds and through its underground rhizomes (root stalks).

Birds

Spring is the time when winter visitors such as fieldfares and redwings leave our shores to head back to Northern Europe. Meanwhile, other birds return to us, having spent winter in warmer countries such as Africa. These include cuckoos, nightingales, wood warblers, swallows and swifts.

One by one, the birds that were quiet or absent during winter sing, joining the resident birds (such as the robin) in a dawn concert that reaches its peak in May.

This cacophony is generally produced by the male birds. Its power indicates what an important time it is for all bird species to establish a territory, find a mate, build a nest and rear young.

Chiffchaff

This migrant warbler is one of the first to arrive to the UK in spring, becoming suddenly plentiful in South England by the end of March. It will sing its name, 'chiffchaff, chiffchaff', from a position high up in a tree, even when it is in the middle of searching for food.

The chiffchaff usually nests close to the ground amid dense shrubbery, in a clumsy ball of dead leaves or moss, bracken and grass; although it will sometimes nest higher in evergreen trees. The female lays around six eggs that are white with dark red spots.

Chiffchaff.

Great tit and blue tit

Two bird species that are numerous in the woodland are the great tit and blue tit, which can regularly be seen darting from branch to branch seeking aphids and other insects to consume. The blue tit is especially good at this, being smaller than the great tit as well as more agile and light; it can hang upside down from a tiny twig if needed. It also eats the seeds from the cones of Scots pines and alder trees. The great tit has a wider diet that also includes acorns and hard nuts that it can hammer with its powerful beak. When foraging, it will feed on the ground more frequently than other species of tits.

The simplest way to tell the two apart (if you don't see them together for size comparison) is by the colour of the tops of their heads: the blue tit has a patch of cobalt blue, while the great tit's cap is entirely black. The great tit also has a distinct, unbroken black line that runs vertically down the front of its chest.

The blue tit's songs consist of multiple variations of a high-pitched 'tsee-tsee', often with a fast trill at the end. The great tit, on the other hand, has a wide range of calls. But the most common and easy to recognise is its two-note 'tee-cher, tee-cher' call. It sings this swinging rusty-metal-gate song so incessantly at this time of year that, for a lot of people, it is synonymous with the arrival of spring.

Blue tit.

Both birds naturally nest within holes in trees. The blue tit will add moss, hair and feathers; the great tit's will be lined with wool or hair. The blue tit lays around eight white eggs that are speckled with red spots at the large end, while the great tit lays up to ten eggs that are similar to the blue tit's, although larger and more heavily spotted.

Long-tailed tit

In spring, the long-tailed tit pair build an egg-shaped nest beautifully made out of tightly-felted moss that is encased with lichen and spiders' webs, and lined inside with feathers. They make the sides of their nest by turning in circles within it, pressing the feathers flat with their breasts. They then add a roof that has a gap for access. The female lays up to twelve pinkish-white eggs with red freckles and, when she is brooding, the end of her long tail will protrude from the gap at the top of the nest. Once the eggs hatch, the pair will sometimes be helped by other long-tailed tits (who do not have nests of their own) in the job of feeding their young.

  THE SECRET LIFE OF A WOODLAND HABITAT

Magpie

It isn't difficult catching sight of a pair of magpies building their sizeable nest at the top of a tree: they make quite a fuss of it. You will notice them repeatedly visiting their chosen site with nest-building materials and, being large and vocal birds, they are hard to miss. They will cement the bottom base of twigs with mud or dung before building the rest of their dome-shaped thorny fortress. The six eggs that are laid are greenish-blue and mottled with grey or brown spots.

Robin

The female robin will create a cup-shaped nest in ivy, a tree stump or even an earth bank, on or close to the ground. She lays up to six white eggs (which have reddish markings) in a clutch, and these hatch after a couple of weeks. The young robins fledge after another two weeks, and do not have the iconic red breast: they start out brown and speckled. Robins can have up to five broods a year.

Dunnock

The inconspicuous dunnock is easily missed in the woodland, with its brown and grey colouring that helps it blend into the background. Although you might observe one singing from a tree, it can usually be seen on the ground or under cover. Its solid nest – hidden in a thick bush or hedge – will be made from moss, fibres and tiny twigs, and lined with wool, hair or feathers. The female lays around five eggs that, in contrast to the bird's subtleties, are a stunning bright blue.

Dunnock.

Wood warbler

Mainly found in oak and beech woods in Wales, western parts of Scotland and North England, from April to September, the attractive wood warbler is yellowy-green with a white chest and under parts. It nests on the ground amongst undergrowth; the nest itself is made of dead leaves, bracken and grass, lined with fine hair and fibres, with a gap in the side. It lays around five to seven eggs that are white and specked with brown.

Nightingale

Despite its plain looks, the brown and cream nightingale is famous, as it has a special song that is complex and full of high and low notes, delivered in fast succession. It can only be found in pockets of Southeast England from April to August, once it has returned from its wintering grounds abroad.

Its name is misleading: it will sing during the daytime as well as at night. However, you will find it difficult to observe, as it tends to hide within dense bushes as it delivers its concert. The female lays four to five brown eggs in spring in a low or ground-level nest formed from leaves and grass.

Greenfinch

The greenfinch, unlike the secretive brown birds previously mentioned, is showy with green and yellow feathers and a drawn-out wheezy 'sweeze' or 'greeen' call. Although it is a resident bird, it is at this time of year that you will start to notice it more frequently within the woodland.

Its nests in bushes and hedges are made of moss, twigs and fibres, and lined with wool and feathers. Its clutch of five to six eggs are pale blue-green with faint red spots and streaks.

Woodpeckers

From winter onwards, woodpeckers will hammer and excavate holes in trees to nest in come spring.

The entrance of the green woodpecker's deep hole is around the size of a tennis ball, with a tunnel that continues horizontally for a few inches before descending at near right angles to an oval chamber that is at least a foot away from the entrance. The bird forgoes nesting material, instead making do with wood chips. It lays up to seven eggs, which are pure white.

The great spotted woodpecker's hole is similarly constructed. It will often use the same tree year after year, but not the same nest. It lays up to six glossy white eggs.

Red kites

In the middle of March, red kites start to build a substantial nest high in a tree on the edge of the woodland, often remaining faithful to the same breeding site each year. Sometimes they will even refurbish last year's nest, or use a squirrel drey or an old buzzard's or crow's nest as a base for their own. The final nest will be around a metre in width, made from long sticks, and up to 40cm deep.

Being large birds, red kites need a route free of obstructing branches in order to access the nest. However, instead of flying directly from sky to nest, they prefer to land on the branch of a nearby tree before taking the last short flight onto the nest. To give themselves a visual guide, or perhaps to warn other kites that the nest is occupied, they will hang unusual items close to or on the edge of the nest, such as pieces of plastic or other rubbish, and even items of clothing that they have purloined.

While soaring the sky, searching for food on the ground below, they will regularly fly over the nest to check on it. Spring sunlight shines golden on their brown feathers, and the white patches on the underside of their wings are lit up. They will issue you with a warning from their curved yellow beaks if you stray too close to their nest site. The red kite pair communicate with each other from a perch or while in the air using a 'weeee-ooh, eee ooh, eee ooh, eee ooh' call.

Red kite on nest.

In April, when egg laying is imminent, the red kites will add the finishing touches to their nest, giving it a soft inner lining of wool and grass. The female lays up to four white eggs (flecked with brown) across one to three days. This will be their only clutch of the year. She will incubate the eggs for the majority of the time, except when the male takes over to allow her to go feed. A month later, the young red kites will hatch at intervals.

The red kite is potentially the UK's most successful reintroduction project so far. Since the release of Swedish, German and Spanish red kites across England and Scotland between 1989 and 2013, these majestic birds have spread across the UK, and can now be found in nearly every English county.

Cuckoo

Looking like a cross between a pigeon and a sparrowhawk, with its blue-grey head and upper parts, barred white under parts and sleek body with pointed wings and long tail, the cuckoo arrives in March and April and stays with us until July (in the case of the adult) or September (in the case of the juvenile). It is generally found in central and southern England and, for many people, summer hasn't really begun until they've heard the first 'coo-coo!' or 'phoo-phoo!'

Male blackbird eating sloe berries in winter.

This sneaky bird is well known for laying its eggs in other birds' nests (often eating an original egg to make space) and leaving the parenting of its young to the unsuspecting owners of the nest. The nest of the dunnock is one of the cuckoo's preferred choices, and it is surprising that the foster parent isn't suspicious of the grey and spotted cuckoo egg amongst its bright blue eggs. When the baby cuckoo hatches, it will eject the remaining eggs or other young from the nest, so that it gets the sole attention of its foster parents.

Blackbird

The male in his smart glossy black outfit starts singing his beautiful song now, which will last well into summer. A warm evening is made dreamy and nostalgic with his elegant song. He will choose a favourite position and sing there at the same time each day.

The brown female is shyer, preferring to remain unnoticed and out of the way. She will continue to forage on the woodland floor, within the undergrowth, until she starts building or rebuilding a nest for their future offspring. The nest can appear in a variety of places: on the ground of a bank or ditch edge, or in a low bush or tree. It is a made out of a wide range of materials, strengthened and lined with mud, with a final soft layer of dry grass. By April, she has probably laid their first clutch of five blue-green eggs with reddish-brown markings – she will lay two or even three further clutches before the year is out.

Insects

As the weather gets milder, overwintering insects wake up to feed, mate and lay eggs – the most eye-catching being the multi-coloured butterflies, whose skipping flight adds to the joyful mood of the season.

Brimstone

This is often the first butterfly you will see in spring. The male butterfly is bright yellow (the female is a paler greenish-yellow) and it therefore stands out as it flits along the still-brown woodland edges and hedgerows. It is believed that the male's original name of 'butter-coloured fly' led to the name now used for this whole group of insects.

Brimstone.

In Tove Jansson's magical novel, *Finn Family Moomintroll*, it is said that if the first butterfly you see in spring is a yellow one, you will have a happy summer. (If you see a white one, it will be a quiet summer.)

This butterfly hibernates through winter as an adult, mates in spring, and then the female lays its eggs on the buckthorn plant. The eggs, caterpillars and pupae are all green and are well camouflaged amongst the spring and summer foliage.

Peacock

Having also hibernated as an adult, the peacock butterfly follows the brimstone, also appearing on warm days in early spring. Look along the hedgerows and woodland edge, and you might find it feeding on the blossom of the blackthorn bush.

It is one of our most strikingly-patterned native butterflies, with its bright red wings that display shimmery blue eye-shapes (reminiscent of the pattern on peacock feathers – hence the name) to ward off predators. A quick flash of these eyes will make a bird think twice about eating it. When at rest with its wings shut, the butterfly is well hidden due to its dark brown underside.

It lays its eggs on stinging nettles in batches of up to 500 and, once hatched a week or two later, the black, spiky polka-dotted caterpillars will feed on this plant. They will emerge as adult butterflies in July, to feed before winter comes.

Peacock on blackthorn blossom.

Small tortoiseshell

Hibernating as an adult amongst leaf litter and in hollow trees, this butterfly also appears in early spring. The tortoiseshell part of the name comes from the yellow and black stripes at the top of the forewings. All four wings are edged with blue half-ovals. Despite these glorious colours, when it is at rest with its wings shut, the butterfly resembles a plain, dead leaf.

The stinging nettle plant is also vital to this butterfly, for egg laying (in batches up to 100), and as food for the black and yellow striped spiny caterpillars. The caterpillars will live together in colonies on the nettles, within protective silken tents.

Orange-tip

The orange-tip butterfly passes winter as a pupa, well disguised amongst the withered vegetation, until it emerges as a butterfly in April and May. The corners of the male's forewings are a vibrant orange, while the female does not have this and so is white apart from her grey wing-tips and two black spots on her forewings. Both are speckled with green on the underside of their hindwings, making for excellent camouflage against sun-dappled foliage. The female lays her eggs on plants such as hedge mustard and lady's smock, which the developing caterpillars feed on before pupating in July.

Comma

Mimicking a crumpled dead leaf while hibernating – with the white comma shape on its underside looking like a crack in the leaf – the comma butterfly spends winter in the open, hanging off branches. In spring, you will notice this orange and brown-black speckled butterfly, with its irregularly-edged wings, enjoying the flowers of the bramble plant.

Comma butterfly.

This butterfly's orange and black striped caterpillars (which have a white patch on the rear) eat stinging nettles as well, but can also be found on hop and currant plants.

Common blue

Emerging in April, the common blue is a widespread butterfly across the UK. The male is a bright blue on the upper side of his wings, while the female is brown. Both have a pale grey-beige underside adorned with black spots ringed in white and an orange tinge along the edge of the wings. Eggs are usually laid twice a year: in June and then again in August or September. The main food plants of the caterpillar are clover, vetch and bird's-foot trefoil.

Holly blue

Also appearing in April, both the male and female holly blue butterflies are blue on their upper sides, although the female has a black border to her wings. Both are pale blue to white underneath, with tiny black dots. This butterfly has two broods per year, with the spring caterpillars feeding on the flowers of the holly tree, and the autumn caterpillars feeding on the buds of ivy, spindle and dogwood.

Speckled wood

Your chances of observing this charming and friendly butterfly along woodland lanes, rides and areas of dappled light are high: it will flit past you, then land on a plant, flower, or the ground. It is less skittish of humans than

Speckled wood.

many other butterfly species, and will obligingly show you its wings, which are brown and speckled with cream dots (some with black and white dots within) – like dappled light on a woodland floor.

The female lays individual white eggs on the grass bordering these places. The green caterpillar (that has darker green and yellow stripes) pupates after ten days, suspended beneath the blades of grass. A second batch of these butterflies will appear during summer.

The speckled wood is unique compared to the other UK butterfly species, in that it can pass winter as a chrysalis or caterpillar, before appearing as an adult the following April.

Ants

Ants become increasingly active in spring, seeking new areas to grow their colony, which will ultimately contain hundreds or thousands of ants. They will choose a place where water and food are within easy reach, in a spot that stays warm at night. They eat insects and other ants, as well as the honeydew that is secreted from the rear ends of aphids and other sap-sucking insects. In order to have this sweet liquid on tap, they will herd aphids into an area that they control, keeping them safe from predators such as ladybirds.

Each colony has at least one queen ant, who will lay her eggs in a brood chamber within the nest. Sterile females maintain the nest, gather food for the colony and feed the larvae with a liquid that they secrete. In summer, clouds of newborn winged females and males will take to the air to mate. Afterwards, the males will die and the impregnated females will shed their wings and look for suitable places to establish a new nest.

The southern wood ant chooses sunny areas in glades and woodland edges for nest sites – especially within coniferous woodlands. It is a large ant at about 1cm in length, with the queen ant around 1.2cm in length. The hairy wood ant, which is found in Northern England, parts of Wales and Scotland, favours similar sites (but also woodland rides) in mixed or coniferous woodland. The Scottish wood ant, on the other hand, can tolerate the shade of dense woodlands.

Ants play an important role within the woodland ecosystem. One service they provide is the dispersal of seeds. For example, they help the spread of the violet, which flowers in spring, by eating the aril part of the plant's seed, and carrying the seed quite a distance from the parent plant before doing so. They also disperse the seeds of the wood anemone.

Ants have a fascinating relationship with blue butterflies, whose caterpillars secrete a liquid that the ants are attracted to. As with aphids, the ants will protect the caterpillars of blue butterflies and feed on the liquid that they secrete. This increases the survival rate of the caterpillars. In the case of the chalkhill blue butterfly, the ants will protect the chrysalis in an underground chamber; the chrysalis emits a chemical and sound that brings the ants to it.

Bees

Of the various species of bee that appear in early spring, many of them are solitary bees that have emerged from their burrows in the ground. They do not sting and are important pollinators for a wide range of flowers and trees. Examples include the early mining bee, the ashy mining bee and the hairy-footed flower bee.

The queens of the bumblebee species (such as tree bumblebees, red-tailed bumblebees and white-tailed bumblebees) are the only members of their colonies to survive winter. They wake up in spring to search for nectar and pollen from early flowers such as dandelions, blackthorn blossom and white dead-nettles (see the photos on pages 13 and 66). They then begin the important work of setting up a new hive.

Bee on blackthorn blossom.

Mammals

Squirrels

After giving birth in March or April, female squirrels will suckle their young for several weeks. At around seven weeks old, the young squirrels have grown fur and opened their eyes, and start to join their mother outside the nursery drey. At ten weeks old, suckling is complete and, armed with their fully-grown teeth, the young move onto solid food.

Deer

Male deer shed their antlers between February and April and begin to grow new ones that will be fully formed, with the velvet shed, by August and September. Therefore in spring, you might be lucky enough to come across some discarded antlers. However, these are usually eaten by the deer to restore their calcium levels.

Male fallow deer, with their growing antlers in velvet.

Hedgehogs

Curled up in their defensive position, hedgehogs will sleep the days away from April to October, venturing out only at night to snuffle noisily along – the grunting sounds leading to the 'hog' part of their name – eating a variety of invertebrates such as beetles, caterpillars, earthworms, slugs and snails. If they chance upon eggs, young birds, frogs, fallen fruit or carrion, they will eat those too. They navigate and find their food using their sense of smell and hearing, as their eyesight is quite poor.

Hedgehogs live for two to three years, although seven isn't unheard of. When they reach sexual maturity at twelve months old, the normally solitary mammals will come together to mate. This usually occurs soon after the hedgehogs have woken from their hibernation. The male will circle the female, snorting and puffing, in a bid to woo her – sometimes seeing off rivals with a head-butt or chase!

Hedgehog © Nick Wilson-Smith.

Badgers

Cubs are now leaving the sett with their extended family, exploring the woodland world and learning the important art of foraging. They will seek out various invertebrates, fallen fruit, small mammals and, most importantly, earthworms; one badger can consume hundreds of earthworms in a single night! A predilection for elderberries means that elder trees are frequently found growing next to badger setts, having passed through the badger's system and self-seeded in the ground there.

Under the cover of darkness, siblings will play and tussle with one another to practise their defence skills and figure out their position in the family hierarchy.

Foxes

Mid-March is when the majority of fox cubs are born. A litter consists of four to five cubs on average, although it can be up to eight. For the first four weeks, cubs are suckled by their mother underground in their natal earth. They then come to the surface to play with one another and to start learning how to forage for earthworms and insects. At this point adults will bring back larger prey, such as birds and mammals, for the cubs to consume as the main part of their diet. The adults are at their lightest during this time, just consuming small mammals, concentrating instead on their parental role.

Pine martens

These chocolate and caramel creatures, with their silky brown bodies and pale apricot throat patches, are classed as critically endangered in England and Wales due to woodland clearance. You are therefore much more likely to encounter them in the pine forests of Scotland, where they exist on an omnivorous diet of berries,

Pine marten.

birds and eggs, small rodents and larger prey, such as hares and grey squirrels. It is believed that their taste for the latter has a positive effect on the number of red squirrels in a woodland habitat, as fewer grey squirrels mean less competition for food and less chance of contracting a fatal disease for the red squirrels. Pine martens themselves are prey to eagles and foxes.

Pine martens are comparable in size to small domestic cats at up to 70cm in length, and they sport an impressive bushy tail. Work is being done to reintroduce these sweet-looking mustelids (they are in the same family as stoats and weasels) to the woodlands in the UK that are missing them.

In spring, female pine martens will give birth to between two and five cubs in March and April, raising them in tree cavities. Six weeks later, the young pine martens will start to leave their nests to explore their woodland home and forage with their mother. In six months' time, they will be fully grown and independent. They will not breed until the summer of their second or third year.

Bats

With temperatures rising in March, bats will begin to emerge from their winter hibernation. However, if there is a cold spell, they can become torpid (inactive) again.

From April, there is much more activity as bats eagerly fill their empty stomachs by feeding nearly every night. Emerging around twenty minutes after sunset, they will hunt on the wing for food such as winged ants and beetles (noctule bats), mosquitos and flies (pipistrelle bats), and midges and moths (noctules and pipistrelles). Brown long-eared bats consume moths, beetles and flies too, but will also eat earwigs and spiders that they glean from woodland foliage. Barbastelle bats mainly eat small moths, as well as some beetles and flies, whereas Bechstein's bats aren't fussy at all, preying on almost all types of insect.

Noctule bats will fly out in the open, well above tree level, with a speedy flight reaching up to 50kph. They repeatedly dive to catch the insects they are chasing. The hunting technique of pipistrelle bats follows a regular pattern, as they move back and forth along the same area. Barbastelle bats forage over a large area and, in summer, will even hunt under the shade of trees during the daytime.

Bechstein's bats listen for insect noise in order to capture their prey. Brown long-eared bats have broad wings and tails, meaning that their flight is highly manoeuvrable, as well as slow and hovering, allowing them to grab insects straight off a leaf.

Come May, female bats will form groups of soon-to-be mothers and will roost together, finding a suitable tree that will become the nursery. Males usually roost separately from the females, on their own or in select groups, although there are some exceptions. For example, a significant proportion of male brown long-eared bats can be found within this bat's maternity roosts.

CHAPTER 3

Summer

Summer is full of heat and flowers
And honeysuckle scent that overpowers.
Yet as buds transform to nut or fruit,
The busy birds fall suddenly mute.

Chloé Valerie Harmsworth

Introduction

At this time of year, the days are hot and sultry. The trees are in full leaf, using the abundant sunshine to synthesise their food. With this extra energy, they will grow fruit from the flowers that have been pollinated.

The butterflies that first appeared in spring are now even more abundant, and others such as the bramble-loving gatekeeper and the majestic purple emperor join in the fun. For many of them, this is the last chance to mate and lay eggs before autumn comes.

Dog-rose.

Each flower is frequented by multi-coloured shining beetles, such as the metallic green swollen-thighed flower beetle. They are feeding and mating, preparing to give birth to the next generation. The honey bee is also visiting the flowers regularly, sipping the precious nectar that will become a delicious liquid encased in the honeycomb of their hive.

Meanwhile, after a busy period of laying eggs and raising young, the woodland birds go quiet as they undergo their annual or bi-annual moult. The silence is filled by singing crickets and grasshoppers in the undergrowth. Secretive snakes and reptiles bask in sunny spots.

Baby mammals born in spring are now learning the ways of the world, usually becoming independent by autumn. In some cases, additional babies are born before the end of summer.

Trees, bushes and plants

In early summer, trees and bushes are thick with colourful flowers, attracting bees, wasps, flies and beetles in their millions. Following pollination through these various sources, the petals of the flowers fall away, and their centres start to swell and transform into fruit. The hawthorn and blackthorn hedges along the woodland edges particularly benefit from the hot summer sunshine that helps to develop their fruit. By the end of summer and into early autumn, these tasty berries will be ready for animals, birds and in-the-know humans to forage.

With trees at peak leaf capacity, the canopy closes up, cutting off the majority of the light from the woodland floor. This suits shade-loving plants and wildflowers, as well as woodland creatures needing respite from the heat. Both will take advantage of these cooler and damper conditions.

Lime flowers
In high summer, the lime tree (also known as linden) bears tiny honey-scented white flowers that will draw clouds of bees to it – making it a tree that you will hear from far away! Once pollinated, the flowers transform into petite green balls that hang from a stem attached to an oval leaf-like sepal. The actual leaves are heart-shaped with saw-toothed edges.

The lime tree can become inundated with aphids, which swarm to suck the sweet sap from the tree. They pass this liquid through their systems, causing anything below to become very sticky!

The honey that bees produce after drinking lime tree nectar is particularly delicious and was traditionally regarded as the finest honey that could be consumed.

Dogwood
This bush is now studded with small black inedible berries.

The bush's bark is rich in tannin and has been used as a substitute for quinine, to treat fever and pain. Historically, soldiers used the leaves in a poultice to cover wounds.

Sweet chestnut
As with the oak, sweet chestnut trees can have a long existence. Five-hundred years is a normal life-span for the tree, although they can live longer. As they reach a grand age, they become progressively misshapen, with gnarled trunks and twisted, heavy limbs that touch the ground.

In June and July, long, thin, yellow catkins appear on the tree. These catkins mainly consist of male flowers, although female flowers appear at their base in sets of three. This is because the tree is monoecious: the flowers of both sexes exist on the same tree.

Sweet chestnut leaves and catkins.

After wind and insect pollination, a protective layer grows over the female parts of the catkins, becoming the spiky green case of the fruit. Inside this, the seeds develop into three glossy brown nuts that are almost triangular in shape – the flat edges being the sides that lie against another nut. The silvery hairs at the point of each are the remains of the stigmas.

Hornbeam

After the last Ice Age over 10,000 years ago, trees from the Continent spread across to our land and colonised it. One of the latecomers was the hornbeam tree which, as pollen records show, only arrived around 5,000 years ago. This was 2,500 years later than the oak tree. The hornbeam predominantly populates woodlands in southern England, frequently appearing alongside the oak.

The hornbeam's trunk of smooth grey bark splits into multiple limbs that extend into a crown that is both symmetrical and densely branched. In winter, its long and pale brown buds are set alternately along the twigs. In April the tree begins to flower just before it comes into leaf. Towards the ends of the twigs, the male and female catkins grow and expand. The male catkins become chains of overlapping yellow-green bracts; the female catkins consist of leafy green bracts that curl up at the tips. The former release pollen from clusters of orange anthers tucked beneath each bract, and the latter have hidden red stigmas waiting to be pollinated.

Hornbeam leaves and wings.

Shortly after come the hornbeam's leaves, which can easily be confused with beech leaves due to their oval shape. The way to tell the two apart is by closer inspection and touch: the edges of hornbeam leaves are sharply toothed, unlike the smooth edges of beech leaves; hornbeam leaves are rough, while beech leaves have a polished feel to them. On top of this, the beech's summer foliage is a darker shade of green than the hornbeam's.

Also in summer, the fertilised female parts of the hornbeam turn into pairs of nutlets within shallow cups. The bracts develop into papery wings consisting of three lobes – the middle one being the longest.

At the end of the season, the tree will start to shed its wings, sending them sailing on the winds that convey the coming of autumn. As well as sowing new hornbeam trees, the nutlets are consumed by squirrels and hawfinches, who take them from the woodland floor or straight from the tree. The green foliage will convert to shades of yellow and ruddy gold before falling to the ground. As with beech trees, however, young hornbeam trees can hold onto their shrivelled brown leaves.

Ferns

From late spring, the curled fronds of ferns arise from the soil of damp, shady woodlands. Protected by brown scales they begin, one by one, to unfurl. Ferns commonly found in this habitat include shield fern, lady fern, male fern, buckler fern and hart's tongue fern. The 'leaves' of these ferns are structured as fronds of ever-dividing leaflets attached to a main stem, with circular scales scattered across the undersides of the leaflets – these are capsules that release the reproductive spores. The exception is hart's tongue, whose 'leaves' are pointed and non-dividing, and bear long straight lines of spore capsules on their undersides. Great variation, however, exists in the appearance and size of ferns, across and within fern species.

Ferns look their best in midsummer, when they are fully unfurled and expanded, covering the woodland floor in a feathery carpet. They look lush and tropical and are evocative of both prehistoric times and exotic climes.

Bracken, another species of fern, can tolerate all soil types including dry and acidic, as well as a wide range of environmental conditions. This makes it a very common sight in woodlands, often growing in extensive stands that have spread due to the plant's underground rhizomes. In autumn, bracken turns an attractive bronze colour, before withering and collapsing in winter. The dried brown fronds that remain

Bracken.

THE SECRET LIFE OF A WOODLAND HABITAT

continue to provide shelter for a multitude of animals, including snakes and small rodents. In spring, before the plant has produced its new green leaves, you may catch sight of shrews dashing between the clumps of dried vegetation. Look closely and you will notice round holes that the beasties have created as entrances into these dwellings, as well as the impressions of miniature paths through these areas, revealing the regular comings and goings.

Bramble

This is the sprawling, fast-growing plant that grows nearly everywhere. Its thorns hint at the fact that this plant is part of the rose family. Indeed, its serrated leaves are very similar to that of the rose.

Each year in spring, shoots grow in arches from the rootstocks before entering the ground to form a new plant, in asexual reproduction.

Although potentially shading out light-loving woodland flowers such as bluebells as they advance across the woodland floor, brambles provide protection for small mammals from predators as well as homes for low-nesting birds. They allow shade-loving plants to grow underneath without being disturbed and provide a habitat for grass snakes. Furthermore, the spread of brambles is kept in check by deer, who eat the leaves.

In early summer, brambles produce white or pale pink five-petalled flowers that are popular with insects and dormice. Post pollination, these flowers turn into the tasty blackberries that are beloved by birds, insects (including the gatekeeper butterfly), humans and other mammals (such as badgers and dormice again). Technically, each juicy segment of a blackberry is a fruit in itself, and so each blackberry is actually a cluster of fruit.

Dog-rose

Another scrambling shrub, with long thorny branches similar to the bramble's, this plant is adorned with sweet-smelling pinky-white flowers in June and July (see the photo on page 70). Reaching up to five metres in height, it is the most abundant wild rose in the UK. By autumn, the flowers have developed into shiny, oval-shaped fruit called rosehips. These treats are eaten by small mammals such as bank voles, as well as by birds. Rosehips are very rich in Vitamin C.

Flowers

Red campion

Appearing in lightly-shaded areas of the woodland in the wake of the bluebells, and growing up to a metre tall, the red campion is another ancient-woodland indicator. With bright pink flowers formed of five petals (each of which has a split, making it look as if there are ten petals), it is an important plant for all sorts of insects, including hoverflies. In traditional medicine, red campion seeds were used to treat snakebites.

Yellow archangel

Also taking over from the bluebell, the flowers of the yellow archangel are hooded and soft yellow in colour, appearing in clusters at intervals up the stalk. The leaves in between the flower sections make it obvious that this plant is part of the dead-nettle family, although they do not sting when you touch them. They grow up to 45cm in height and you can find them in the woodland from May to June.

Yellow archangel.

Honeysuckle

Spiralling in a clockwise direction up the stems of bushes and trees, this climbing plant can reach up to 7 metres in height. Flowering from June to September, the honeysuckle's wonderful scent is particularly potent on warm summer evenings. Formed of two lips and a slender tube, its flowers can only be pollinated by moths and bees with long tongues (proboscises). The flowers are initially a cream or yellow colour, before becoming orange with a hint of crimson after pollination. The flowers then develop into clusters of red berries. The oval leaves appear as opposite pairs, with smooth, non-toothed edges.

Foxglove

A biennial plant, the handsome foxglove will appear in its first year as a rosette of downy leaves that aren't too dissimilar to those of the primrose or cowslip. It is not until the second year – from June to September – that the flower spike is produced, reaching as high as 2 metres in height. Hanging from one side of this stem are tubular purple-pink flowers, with dark spots at their entrances to guide the bees that crawl in to drink the nectar, pollinating the flowers with pollen from other foxgloves as they do so.

The thousands of miniscule seeds released from this plant result in drifts of foxgloves, especially in open spaces where felling or coppicing has occurred, and along the edges of the woodland. Some people believe that these plants can be found close to fox dwellings, and this might be one reason for its name.

'Digitalis' in its scientific name refers to the finger-like shape of the flowers. Other names include witches' gloves and dead men's bells – referring to the fact that it is toxic. Although poisonous if consumed directly, the plant contains a chemical that can treat those suffering from high blood pressure or heart conditions.

Cow parsley

Shade-loving cow parsley has distinctly parsley-shaped, feathery leaves. From April to June, its sprays of frothy white flowers appear in umbrella-like clumps, and are popular with insects such as bees, hoverflies and orange-tip butterflies. The plant has a long history of being used as a mosquito repellent. It is a member of the carrot family.

Cow parsley.

Dog's mercury

This perennial plant is particularly prevalent in beech and oak woodlands, and other shady places. It spreads through its underground rhizomes, forming a carpet of plants where it grows. It is related to wood spurge and its leaves were once used to make a dye. Its shoots appear in spring, and by early summer, flowers appear at the base of the leaves, just like those of nettles. The male flowers are tiny and yellow.

Birds

By early summer, swifts, swallows and other birds have returned. Baby birds – even those that have left the nest – are fed worms and caterpillars by their doting parents. The male blackbird serenades us with his song and the female lays another clutch of eggs. Speckled young robins and other young birds are learning how to sing.

Bullfinch

The bullfinch is a charming bird that isn't too dissimilar from the chaffinch, except that it has a black head instead of grey, and this appears on both sexes. The male has an orange-pink breast, whereas the female's is buff in colour. In spring, the bullfinch pair will have raised up to five chicks in a nest made of twigs, moss, lichen and fine roots, 1.2–2.1 metres off the ground.

Unfortunately, although the bullfinch was once popular as a captive bird due to its lovely looks and call, its numbers have declined considerably in the UK. This is due to various factors including the reduction in size and diversity of its scrub and woodland habitat, as well as agricultural intensification.

Further to this, it can be difficult to spot them during summer, as they are quiet in their behaviour and not very gregarious. It is believed that they stay as a pair throughout the year, although they will sometimes travel in small flocks.

Turtle dove

Smaller and daintier than collared doves and wood pigeons, the turtle dove is very rare across the UK. The reason is believed to be a shortage of food during their breeding season, leading to fewer turtle doves being born. Their comforting purring call can, however, be heard from the tops of trees on the woodland edges at Knepp

Turtle dove at Knepp Estate.

Estate in West Sussex, where their numbers are rising. It is thought that this could be due to the introduction of Tamworth pigs on site (see pages 94 and 95), whose rootling activities have led to the turtle dove's food plants, such as red fescue, growing in larger amounts.

You can distinguish the turtle dove from other doves and pigeons not just by its call, but also by the mottled brown and black colouring on its wings. Having arrived on our shores between April and May, the turtle doves will leave again between August and September.

Tree sparrow

The tree sparrow is another example of a scarce and declining bird. Both sexes look the same, with mahogany heads, black cheek spots and black and brown backs and wings. Mating for life, the tree sparrow nests in tree holes, producing as many as three broods of seven eggs each year. It eats insects, seeds and weeds.

The moult

After a busy spring of laying eggs and an early summer spent raising chicks (and then feeding fledglings), birds undergo a moult of their feathers at the end of the summer season. Because of this, it can seem as if a silence has suddenly descended upon the woodland. Birds go quiet as they shed their old, worn-out feathers and grow strong new ones, which they will need when winter comes. They will also try to stay out of sight. This is partly due to their energy being focused on the moult, leaving little for moving about. Depleted plumage means that they are less able to fly. This leaves them vulnerable to attack from predators. Hence, they try not to draw attention to themselves, and rest as much as possible.

At the same time, the newly-fledged birds lose their first set of feathers and moult into their adult coats. For example, juvenile robins shed their spotty body feathers, which are replaced with the recognisable brown and orange feathers to match the adults.

Once their moult is complete, the birds that came to the UK for the summer prepare to return to warmer countries, such as Africa and Spain.

Anting

As well as their once or twice-yearly moult, birds need to regularly service their feathers to keep them pristine. One way in which they do this is by using the anting technique. Anting involves the bird crouching atop of a nest of non-stinging ants and letting the insects crawl over its plumage. The ants, aware of an invader, release their defensive chemicals onto the bird's feathers in an attempt to protect their colony. As these chemicals are toxic, it is likely that this 'ant shampoo' will kill parasites and pests living on the bird. In some cases, the bird will pick up the ants and rub them onto its feathers rather than passively letting them do the job. Either way, the bird then preens itself and removes the dead insects. Other theories are that the ants' acid may supplement the bird's natural preening oil, or that by rubbing the ants against its feathers, the bird removes their distasteful acid and can subsequently eat the ants. Some birds carry out this activity during their moulting period, so perhaps it also helps to stimulate the growth of new feathers. Substitutes such as snails, wasps, millipedes and grasshoppers are sometimes used.

Insects

In summer, butterfly numbers reach their peak, and dragonflies, damselflies, bees, beetles and other insects are abundant.

Butterflies and moths

Purple emperor

In June and July, especially in southern England, this magnificent butterfly can be observed flying high above oak trees, battling rival males and finding obliging females. Occasionally they will visit the ground to drink from a puddle or feed upon pungent fox poo. The males of this species have an attractive deep purple sheen on the upper side of their wings; the females meanwhile look similar to white admirals. The underside of both sexes are a mix of orange, white, black and brown. Eggs are laid on sallow (willow) and will stay there until the following spring, when the large green horned caterpillar will feed on the tree's leaves.

Red admiral.

Red admiral

The red admiral is a brown-black butterfly, with a distinctive red stripe across the forewings and along the edge of the hindwings, and the addition of white spots in the corners of the forewings. Buddleia bushes are one of the butterfly's favourites for nectar, and in autumn it feeds on rotting fruit. The red admirals that we see at the end of summer and in early autumn are the offspring of the red admirals that migrated here from the Mediterranean in spring. The caterpillar feeds on stinging nettles.

White admiral

This blackish-brown butterfly with white bands can be found across the UK, but especially in the south of England. Its larva feeds on honeysuckle and passes winter in a shelter made from spinning the edges of a leaf together, secured with silk to a stem.

Gatekeeper

This brown and orange butterfly is very common in summer, and can be seen enjoying the flowers of blackberry (bramble) bushes. Appropriately, another name for it is the hedge brown. The male and female are nearly identical in appearance and both have a black dot in the top corner of their forewings (with two white dots

Gatekeeper.

inside it). One slight difference is the presence of a dark bar of scent scales on the male's forewings. This butterfly looks similar to the meadow brown, which only has one white dot within the black dot on its forewing. However, the gatekeeper is smaller and a more vibrant orange, and tends to hold its wings open when at rest.

Brown hairstreak

The largest of our native hairstreak butterflies, the brown hairstreak lives in open woodland and can be discerned flitting around trees, where it mates and feeds upon aphid honeydew. It will also feed on brambles and wildflowers. The female lays white eggs on blackthorn shoots, so that the larvae can feed on them once they hatch the following spring. Both sexes are brown, but the female has a large orange patch on her forewings while the male does not. The two wavy white lines that give this butterfly its name can be seen on the underside of its wings when it closes them at rest.

Purple hairstreak

As its scientific name *Favonius quercus* indicates, this butterfly is loyal to the oak (quercus) tree. The male purple hairstreak's forewings are covered all over with a purple-blue sheen, and the female has a patch of indigo on her forewings. This butterfly will fly around the outer branches of oaks, enjoying honeydew and laying its eggs on the tree so that its larvae can feed upon the leaves. Incredibly elusive, it only comes to ground level in search of nectar and water when there is a prolonged drought.

Painted lady

In July, crowds of this butterfly migrate to our shores from North Africa, and some years will see record numbers of them come to the UK. The painted lady favours the buddleia bush – on which you will most likely view it – but it feeds on thistle, viper's bugloss, mallow and nettles too.

Elephant hawk-moth

This stunning olive green and hot pink moth flies on summer nights, feeding on the flowers of honeysuckle plants, on which it will rest during the day. Its chunky brown caterpillar (which has snake-like eye spots) can extend its foremost segments into a shape reminiscent of an elephant's trunk, thus giving the butterfly its name. The caterpillar eats plants such as willowherb, fuchsia and bedstraw.

Cinnabar moth

Look for the bright yellow ragwort plant in summer and, chances are, you will find the caterpillar of the cinnabar moth. These striking caterpillars are striped with bands of orange and black, and will swarm the ragwort, which is their food. The brightly coloured and patterned caterpillar turns into an equally impressive moth – one with scarlet hindwings and black forewings marked with a scarlet stripe and two scarlet dots.

Six-spot burnet moth

Another eye-catching black and red moth, patterned with six red spots on each forewing, the six-spot burnet can be found on flowers such as knapweed, scabious and thistle. Its larvae live and feed on vetches, clovers and other low-lying plants, such as bird's-foot trefoil.

Large thorn moth

This moth flies at the end of summer and into autumn. It is quite scarce. The larvae of this amber-coloured moth feed on trees such as birch and hawthorn, looking like grey-brown twigs or thorns.

THE SECRET LIFE OF A WOODLAND HABITAT

Six-spot burnet moth.

Dragonflies and damselflies

Within the woodland, especially where there is water, you can catch sight of dragonflies and damselflies darting through the air, shining with extraordinary jewel colours. Dragonflies can be found further from water since they are strong fliers.

To tell the difference between the two, observe them at rest on a perch: dragonflies will sit with their wings open; damselflies will fold their wings together. The latter are delicate and slender compared to the larger, stockier dragonflies. Furthermore, dragonflies' eyes touch, whereas those of damselflies are separate. There are fifty-seven species of dragonfly in the UK and twenty-one species of damselfly.

Both dragonflies and damselflies eat insects such as midges and are predated by birds and frogs. Their presence indicates oxygen-rich, unpolluted water, which is essential for their breeding. If you spy one dipping the lower half of its body into water, you are witnessing the female laying eggs! A week later the eggs will hatch into nymphs, who slowly develop underwater into their adult form, eating aquatic larvae while they do so. The nymphs are predated by amphibians and fish.

Large red damselflies laying eggs.

Look out for the robust broad-bodied chaser dragonfly that flies from April to September. Around 5cm in length, the male has a blue abdomen with yellow spots down the sides, while the female has a golden abdomen and paler spots. It may regularly come to rest on a favourite stem, for example on a blackthorn bush, leaving to catch its flying food before returning to the same place.

Perched on a leaf of the wild cherry tree might be a black and ruby beauty called the large red damselfly, which flies from the end of April through to August.

Hovering around the ditches and ridges that have filled with rainwater, and hunting along woodland rides, is the southern hawker. With acid green and bright blue sections against a dark background, this dragonfly catches the eye not just because of its large size (reaching 7cm in length). This is a dragonfly that has no fear of humans, often coming very close.

Male broad-bodied chaser dragonfly.

Bees and hoverflies

Bees are eagerly collecting pollen and nectar from the summer flowers. The honey bee in particular is performing an important role – not just of pollination, but in the service of its hive.

Honey bees

Honey bee hives consist of a queen, sterile female worker bees and male drones. A hive that is doing well can have as many as 80,000 individuals. The hive is constructed from hexagonal cells of wax secreted by the workers that are built up into a series of combs. Within some of the wax cells, pollen is stored for food; others are used for rearing young or to contain the bees' honey (which is regurgitated nectar from flowers). From the thousands of eggs laid by the queen, only one will have been chosen to become the new queen. This one is given extra-special treatment, including a larger cell to grow in and a feed of royal jelly (from the workers' special glands), right up until she is fully developed.

On a summer's day in the woodland, swarms of honey bees can sometimes be seen. This is the old queen being followed by worker bees – they will fill the air or gather together as a crawling mass on a branch, until a site is found to set up a new hive. Meanwhile, the new queen remains with the old hive. She will fly out to be impregnated by one of the male drones in mid-air, before returning to the hive.

Hoverflies

At a time when aphids could gobble up millions of leaves, interfering with trees' creation of nutrients from sunlight, hoverflies come to the rescue. These black and yellow insects mimic bees and wasps to put off those

Hoverfly.

that would otherwise prey on them. In their hovering flight, they visit and pollinate flowers, and locate aphid colonies through scent. They will then lay 100 eggs a day, up into the thousands, and these eggs will hatch just a few days later. The emerging larvae capture the aphids, piercing them with their hook-like mouthparts and sucking out their insides.

Over the course of ten or so days, the hoverfly larvae grow and consume up to 800 aphids each. The ants who farm the aphids for the honeydew they excrete will attempt to fight off the hoverfly larvae, but are deterred by the slime that they exude in response. Once full-grown, the hoverfly larvae attach themselves to leaves or twigs and turn into pupae and, after a further ten days, leave their cases as adult hoverflies. Hoverflies can go through several generations of this process before autumn arrives, at which point the larvae will shelter in the soil and not become pupae until the following spring.

Beetles

Stag beetle
If you live in the south-east of England, look out for this beast of a beetle in your woodland. At 3–5cm in length, with impressive 'antlers' on the male that are in fact its jaws, this rare beetle can be found (if you're lucky)

amongst undisturbed rotting wood between May and August. It can also be glimpsed on courtship flights, making a droning sound, on warm summer evenings.

It takes years of the large white larva feeding on dead wood underground before it can emerge as an adult – to live for a mere few weeks. During this short time, it lives mainly on the fat reserves it built up as a larva. The male's deadly-looking jaws are used to fight its rivals in order to win a female; it wrestles rather than bites with these. After mating, the female will return to the site of her emergence, dig down into the soil and lay thirty or so eggs.

Sadly, it is now quite a rare beetle, due to the shrinking and disappearance of woodland areas and the dead wood it relies on being cleared away. It is one of only three species of stag beetles in the UK; the others are the rhinoceros beetle and the lesser stag beetle.

Soldier beetle

Look at the thistles and umbellifer plants such as hogweed and wild carrot that are growing in the glades, rides and at the edges of your woodland in July and August – there's a very good chance that they will be frequented, in considerable numbers, by soldier beetles. Long and thin and in a variety of colours, the soldier beetles wait on flowers for the insects that they prey on, or a mate, to visit. They also partake in the nectar and pollen of the flowers.

The red soldier beetle is one of the most common of the soldier beetles, and you can recognise it by its red-orange colouring and black tip.

Violet ground beetle

From the hundreds of ground beetle species we have in the UK, this is one of the most attractive. At 3–4cm in length, this flightless black beetle with a purple sheen and violet edges moves quickly across the woodland floor at night, searching for slugs, caterpillars, worms and other invertebrates to consume. During the day it will hide under leaf litter, amongst log piles and under stones. Its larva actively hunts too, and has the same diet.

Red-headed cardinal beetle.

Red-headed cardinal beetle

This 2cm long bright red-orange beetle with black legs and long toothed antennae loves to bask on leaves, flowers and tree trunks in the heat of the sun. It eats other, smaller insects. The female lays her eggs under the bark of dead wood. When the larvae hatch, they will stay under the bark of dead or even living trees, and feed on the larvae of other insects before pupating.

Similar beetles include the scarcer black-headed cardinal beetle and the lily beetle. The first can be identified by its black head and darker red wing cases; the latter has a black head too, but is rounder in shape and has a dimpled texture to its wing cases.

7-spot ladybird

The classic beetle that a lot of people are familiar with is the ladybird. There are over forty species of ladybird, although only twenty-six can be visibly recognised as such. These twenty-six species are named after the number of spots on their wing cases.

The female 7-spot ladybird emerges from her hibernation in March and April, and lays groups of pointy yellow or orange eggs on leaves and plant stems in June and July.

Once hatched, the spiky brown-grey larvae with orange splotches will aggressively hunt and feast on aphids. This is the favourite food of the adult ladybirds too, who suck out the aphids' insides through the aphids' rear ends. During the year in which the adult lives, it will eat as many 5,000 aphids.

Birds usually avoid eating ladybirds, as the beetle's bright colouring indicates toxicity. It is, however, predated by spiders and other, larger beetles.

Swollen-thighed flower beetle

Also known as the thick-legged flower beetle, this common and widespread beetle with long and elegant antennae, is an eye-catching metallic green. It is a hue that gleams particularly bright on hot, sunny days.

Swollen-thighed flower beetle (male).

Only the male possesses the bulbous thighs (femora) that give the beetle its name. It can be found in woodland clearings on a wide range of open-structured flowers including daisies, cornflowers and cow parsley. Its larvae live and feed in the hollow stems of plants.

Leaf-rolling and nut-boring weevils

There are a few weevils – which are essentially beetles with long snouts – that cut up and roll the ends of leaves to form a protective home around the single eggs they have laid. The larva will grow inside this leafy shell and consume the inner part of its home before turning into a pupa. Once it has transformed into its beetle shape, it will bite its way out. One example is the oak-leaf roller, which has a reddish brown body and black head. They are amongst our largest weevils, at 5–8mm in length. They generally live on the foliage of young oaks, but can be found on beech and birch trees too.

There are also weevils that burrow into the nuts of trees, such as the hazelnut weevil, that has a scaly yellow-brown body and rusty-coloured legs. In May and June, the adult weevils feed on hawthorn flowers. Then, in early summer, the female will seek out a hazel tree to set up her nursery. She will bore deep into a young green hazelnut using her long snout, before depositing a single egg there. The egg will turn into a larva that will spend the summer feeding on the nut kernel while it grows. Once the nut falls to the ground in autumn, the larva will gnaw its way out of the shell (leaving a neat round hole) and burrow into the safety of the soil to spend winter. It will emerge as an adult weevil the following spring.

Grasshoppers and crickets

With eleven species of grasshopper and twenty-three species of cricket in the UK, there are too many to mention them all, so here are just two examples. To tell grasshoppers and crickets apart, the simplest thing to do is to look at their antennae: the grasshopper's is short; the cricket's is long.

Presiding in woodland rides during summer, the common green grasshopper is up to 2.3cm in length, and is mostly green, although it sometimes has brown sides. To woo females, the male will make music by rubbing his legs against comb-like structures on his forewings. This song lasts around twenty seconds and sounds similar to the free-spinning wheels of a bicycle. After mating, the female lays her eggs in the soil, which will hatch the following April. The newborn grasshoppers will then reach maturity by June, ready to begin the cycle all over again.

The oak bush-cricket lives, breeds and feeds exclusively in trees. Its preferred habitat is in warm ancient woodlands, ideally with numerous oak trees. You will have trouble observing it as it spends much of its time hidden in the canopy of the mature trees (which it can jump between), and is very well camouflaged: its lime-green colouring matches the leaves exactly. Furthermore, it is tiny, at around 1.5cm. It has an orange-yellow stripe down its back and feeds on invertebrates such as caterpillars and other larvae (it is predominantly carnivorous, unlike most other bush-crickets). To draw females to him, the male oak bush-cricket drums his hind legs on the leaves. The female lays her eggs individually in lichen, moss and the bark of trees. The nymphs hatch from these in spring, before reaching maturity in July and August.

Reptiles and amphibians

Snakes and reptiles favour the grassy edges of the woodland, where they can be found sunbathing. However, they are secretive and shy creatures, and will quickly take cover in dense undergrowth if disturbed. Within woodlands, especially those that have water, they will live under bracken and other vegetation.

Grass snake.

Grass snake

Growing to an impressive length of up to 150cm, the grass snake is the longest snake in the UK. It is olive grey or brown in colour, with a yellow or orange band around its neck and vertical black lines along its sides. Harmless to humans, it eats aquatic wildlife such as toads, frogs, fish and newts in the wet places where it prefers to reside. It hibernates from October to April.

In summer, the female grass snake lays up to 40 eggs in rotting vegetation and incubates them until they hatch in autumn.

The grass snake is an excellent swimmer and can quickly slither into nearby water when disturbed. Another tactic it uses to avoid predation from birds and mammals such as badgers and foxes is to play dead – presumably making itself a less appealing snack. It can also release a foul-smelling substance from its anal gland to deter attackers. Grass snakes can live for up to twenty-five years.

Adder

The grey-brown adder is the only venomous snake in the UK; however, it hides from humans in undergrowth, rarely delivering its bite, which is hardly ever lethal. This handsome creature reaches up to 80cm in length and has red eyes. It hibernates from October to March. When not sunbathing on logs or under warm rocks in woodland glades on sunny days, the adder will hunt lizards, ground-nesting birds and small mammals. In summer, the female incubates her fertilised eggs internally, before giving birth to up to twenty live young. The adder can live for up to fifteen years.

Adder.

Slow worm

Even though this shiny and smooth creature looks like a snake, it is in fact a legless lizard. Harmless to humans, this reptile – that can reach up to 50cm in length – leaves its hiding place under a stone or log to search for slugs, snails, earthworms and insects at dusk or after rain. As with the famous chameleon of sunnier climes, the slow worm can drop its tail to escape when threatened. This brown-grey lizard (the males of which sometimes sport scattered blue spots) can live for up to twenty years. It hibernates under tree roots or piles of leaves from October to March. In summer, it will sunbathe in the warm weather, and the female – who has a dark line along her back – will give birth to around eight young.

Common lizard

As its name suggests, the common lizard can be found all over the UK. Reaching up to 15cm in length, it is usually brown-grey (though it can vary in colour) with rows of spots or stripes down its sides and along its back. The sexes can be told apart by their bellies: the female has a pale, plain belly, while the male has a vibrant orange or yellow belly with spots. As with the slow worm, the common lizard can shed its tail – which will continue to move – when escaping an attacker. It can then regrow this tail, although the new one won't be as long as the original. The common lizard hibernates from October to March before emerging in spring to mate in April and May. The female incubates her young internally before giving birth to up to eleven young in July. The common lizard eats flies, spiders, insects and other inverrebrates, and lives for up to six years.

Common frog and toad

Woodlands that have ponds or rainwater-filled ditches are home to the common frog and the common toad. The first is a mottled yellow, green or brown, and has moist skin that is smooth in texture, and a brown patch behind its eyes. Adults can be up to 9cm long. The latter is grey-brown, has dry, warty skin and can be up to 10cm long. Another way to tell them apart is in the way they move: frogs leap and jump; toads crawl. The common frog can normally be found in damp habitats close to fresh water, while the common toad is better able to live in dry environments. It will, however, travel a long way to return to its breeding grounds, following its strong migratory instinct. Both need water to lay their eggs in, with toads preferring deeper ponds. Frogspawn is laid in clumps, and toadspawn, which appears a few weeks later, takes the form of long strings. These eggs develop into tadpoles before growing legs and leaving the water, usually in June, but sometimes as late as September. Frogs eat snails and slugs; toads eat ants – but both will eat beetles, woodlice and bugs. The toad in particular hunts at night.

Common frog.

Newts

Out of the three native species of newt in the UK, the smooth (or common) newt is the one you are most likely to encounter in a woodland.

The smooth newt, which is grey-brown with an orange underside speckled with black spots, hibernates amongst tree roots or underground in woodlands from October to around March. When the male mates in spring, he has a smooth crest running along his back and tail. When on land, the smooth newt feeds on the invertebrates (such as caterpillars) it finds in the hedgerows and woodland; when in water, it eats tadpoles, molluscs and crustaceans. It is most active at night. The female lays individual eggs that are carefully wrapped in a pond weed leaf. Unlike frogs and toads, the newt larvae develop their front legs first. They live underwater until they lose their gills, leaving in late summer to reside in damp, sheltered places. The smooth newt grows up to 10cm long.

Mammals

Shrews

Common and pygmy shrews are active both day and night, and at this time of year their high-pitched squeaks can be heard as they fight over territories.

Stoats and weasels

Having had their litter of kits in spring, stoats will mate again during the summer season. However, the fertilised eggs do not implant until the next spring. This year's young were born deaf, blind and naked, four weeks after implantation. It will take twelve weeks (during which they will be fed by their mother) to grow and learn how to be efficient hunters. The stoat usually stays in ditches and hedgerows – especially when hunting its smaller prey – and will search areas by running in a zig-zag pattern. However, you might witness the rare appearance of a stoat out in the open, delivering its deadly bite to the back of a larger mammal's neck, such as a rabbit's.

Weasel.

The female weasel will have given birth to up to six young in spring, and these will be weaned within four weeks, ready to hunt at just eight weeks. When hunting, the weasel generally keeps to the runways and tunnels of small rodents such as voles and mice, which are its main food. It can even use these routes during winter, moving underneath snow if necessary. If there aren't enough voles or mice about, it can eat bird's eggs and baby rabbits instead. In years when food is abundant, the female can have two litters.

Squirrels

A month after they have stopped suckling, the young grey squirrels will leave their mother to build dreys of their own. Their mothers may give birth to another litter in August, but the female young will not breed until next year.

In summer, the grey squirrel's fur turns to a yellowish brown. The red squirrel's fur can bleach to various shades of cream.

Deer

Both roe and red deer now wear bright rusty red coats.

Female roe deer will give birth to a single calf or twins between May and July, after an eight to ten month gestation period. For the first six weeks of their life, calves are adorably spotted on their flanks, providing excellent camouflage as they rest and hide amongst vegetation in dappled woodland.

The roe deer's breeding season, or 'rut', occurs from mid-July to mid-August. The bucks will fight aggressively, sometimes to the death, over territories and does (female deer). Victorious bucks will chase a doe until she is willing to mate; does will attract bucks with a high-pitched piping call. The fertilised egg will not implant or start growing until January, and then foetal growth takes five months, and so winter births are avoided. This is unique to this deer species.

Female fallow deer give birth to a single fawn in June or July, under the cover of long grass or bracken; female red deer give birth to a single fawn from mid-May to mid-July.

Hedgehogs

Thirty-five days after impregnation, in early to late summer, female hedgehogs will give birth to a litter of between three to seven hoglets. These are born naked; however, it doesn't take long for them to grow a coat of white spines, which are later replaced by their adult spines.

While mother hedgehog is suckling her children, she may sometimes leave the nest in the late afternoon to gather nesting material or extra food.

Sadly, only two to three hoglets tend to survive, and once suckling and a short period of going out with their mother on foraging trips is over, these individuals are ready to become independent.

Although females can have a second litter in September or October, these hoglets are generally unable to put on enough weight in time for hibernation and so do not make it through winter.

Wild pigs and boar

Although they were hunted to extinction in the thirteenth century, wild boar can now again be found in certain UK woodlands, such as in Kent and the Forest of Dean. After escaping farms where they were bred for their meat, they have since been expanding their numbers and their range. Although their tusks and substantial size can make them rather intimidating in appearance, wild boar are actually very shy and usually nocturnal creatures.

In several places across the UK, pigs are being used to carry out the role that wild boar would have previously played. At Knepp Estate in West Sussex, Tamworth pigs (which are believed to be descended from an indigenous

THE SECRET LIFE OF A WOODLAND HABITAT

Tamworth pig foraging in the woodland at Knepp Estate.

species) are allowed to roam the woodlands freely. These attractive, gingery pigs snuffle for roots, grubs, berries and nuts to eat, under the soil and amongst the leaf litter. In doing so, they provide the necessary space for seeds to grow and invertebrates to burrow. They also expose further seeds for birds and other animals to eat. The woodland wildlife also appreciates the muddy wallows that the pigs create.

Badgers

On warm days, badgers may leave their sett slightly earlier, just before sunset. In July and August, the adults have begun to mate again. The young badgers who were born in February will be feeding independently by now, venturing above ground to hunt and play.

Foxes

In early June, fox cubs will begin to leave their natal earth, unless the weather has been particularly hot – in which case they will abandon it earlier. They will now hide in dense cover above ground, such as in bramble patches. Initially, they will follow the adults' cues as to what is worth sniffing and what is worth hunting – starting with easy prey, such as earthworms and insects.

In July, the cubs are further developing their hunting skills. Although they will still go for easier prey such as earthworms and insects, they are now able to feed themselves and will start to compete with the adults for more substantial food. August will see them becoming increasingly independent.

Badger © Nick Wilson-Smith.

Bats

In June, one tiny pup per female bat will be born. Pups will stay in the all-female roost for three to six weeks, suckling their mother's milk. After this time, some will start learning to fly and catch their own insects. Once the pups have gained their independence, the maternity colonies will disperse, ready for autumn's mating season.

THE SECRET LIFE OF A WOODLAND HABITAT

CHAPTER 4

Autumn

Autumn replaces the sun-dried summer
With discarded leaves the colours of treasure.
The edible jewels adorning the bushes and trees
Along with golden sunsets,
Are a bounty beyond measure.

Chloé Valerie Harmsworth

Introduction

After the exuberance of spring and the headiness of summer, it can seem – to the casual observer, at least – as if nature is slowing down in autumn. Not a bit of it. Although the assumption might be that there isn't much to notice in the natural world other than a short but stunning display of vibrant yellow, red and orange leaves, there is more to autumn than this. Yes, many of our native birds will have flown (or will soon fly) to warmer climes, and the majority of the wildflowers will have transformed into dry stalks and seedheads, but there is still a lot going on in the woodland.

In fact, this season rivals spring as the most industrious period of the year – for our birds and mammals especially. Some are preparing to sleep away winter, while others are frantically gathering resources to see them through a time when it will be a lot harder to find sustenance.

This is a fantastic time of year for an invigorating walk through woodlands. On sunny days in early autumn, you can almost be fooled into thinking that it's still summer, with tiny spiders floating on a soft breeze, held aloft by their silken parachutes. They are searching for a new home. Certain butterflies such as the speckled wood can still be glimpsed flitting down woodland rides and through dappled glades. Flies are mating on the ground and not all the insects have died or hidden themselves away just yet.

By the end of autumn, the light changes and softens, with an evening-like quality all day – the reddening orb hanging increasingly low in the sky. Any remaining blue flowers stand out vibrantly in this light and against the glow of a goldening background. A burnt smell slowly builds in the woodland as old wood and leaves decay, releasing chemicals that create the classic 'autumnal' scent.

The ground is damper and the air is cooler. There is a banging coming from the hazel copse: the coppicer is carrying out his autumn tasks, or perhaps it's the sound of squirrels and jays breaking open their pilfered hazelnuts. Piles of large yellow-green sycamore leaves glow against dark brown soil, as evenings draw in.

Having discovered the minute woodland miracles of the previous seasons, you can now delve into the details of this magical time. Take the time to appreciate autumn's beautiful changes. You will be surprised and enthralled at what you find.

Autumn woodland with bracken.

Foraging

As easy as it is to wish that the warmth of summer would never end, autumn comes with a multitude of rewards. As the days and nights cool, it is time to prepare for winter. One way to do this is to forage for nature's edible treasures.

Innately, this ancient practice feels correct; it feels right. And yet it can feel transgressive. Despite it having been a normal activity for many people up until fairly recently in history, today it can be met by others with confusion, surprise and possibly even suspicion.

Sadly, in the main, foraging is a forgotten art. It has been lost over time as humans moved away from the woodlands, and with the growth of towns and cities. Living in urban environments has changed the majority of human lifestyles and, as a result, most people have lost their connection with the natural world. And with this disconnection, once common knowledge is no longer being passed down the generations. What was once well-known is now generally unknown, and the unknown shouldn't be trusted.

However, there are people who respect it, impressed that food and drink can be made and flavoured with ingredients sourced from our local woodlands. Some of these people remember their father or grandfather

Elderberries.

making elderberry wine, their mother making elderflower cordial and their grandparents brewing beer and infusing gin with sloes.

Foraging is an incredibly enjoyable pastime in autumn. It is possible to spend hours happily reaching into thickets of tangled branches, plucking juicy berries, with stained hands and scratched fingers. Deep in the woodland, you can enjoy shafts of soft sunlight falling between the gaps in the trees, delicately touching the ground and lighting up the various shades of yellow, orange, red and green of the deepening layer of leaves.

When you are engrossed in this mindful gathering activity, you can think about what you will make with your treasures, while simultaneously taking in the minutiae of the moment: blackbirds scrabbling at the base of trees, riffling through the mulch; red kites calling overhead and a robin eyeing you curiously from a nearby branch.

By foraging, you can take a break from our society's relentless rhythm of emails, phone calls, cars and central heating, and get outside. By tapping back into this ancient activity and natural awareness, you will get to know the seasons better and the life cycle of plants, and no longer fear the growing darkness that follows summer. One thing always follows another, and humans are a part of that. By rediscovering these skills, you will access your deeper and more essential self. By practicing sustainable methods utilised by people for thousands of years, you are communing with your ancestors.

This chapter mentions some of the fruits and nuts worth foraging in autumn. Remember that you should always check that you have permission to forage and make sure you are confident in what you are picking, to avoid toxic berries and plants. Finally, the rule of thumb is to only forage what is already abundant and to leave plenty behind for other foragers and wildlife. On the trees and bushes you pick from, pick from the middle, as this will leave the bounty at the top for the birds and the bounty at the bottom for badgers, deer and other animals. This also gives the trees and bushes the chance to drop their fruit to the ground, to germinate there, or to be transferred further afield by the animals who eat them.

Trees, bushes and plants

The most recognisable indicator of autumn, that nobody can miss, is the leaves changing colours and falling, one by one, onto the sodden or frosty ground. The leaves of the cherry trees are turning orange and the keys of the field maple trees are yellowing. The colour changes occur when trees draw the green chlorophyll from their leaves back into their trunks, leaving behind the other pigments. The trees then shed these leaves, which won't photosynthesise and produce food for them during the darker winter months. No longer having leaves to pass nutrients to saves much-needed energy for the trees.

The fallen leaves decompose on the woodland floor, releasing nutrients back into the soil. Much of this work is done by earthworms, who pull fallen leaves underground to partially consume – the rest is left to rot. Fungi, bacteria and creatures such as mites, woodlice, millipedes, beetles and springtails also play an important role in breaking down fallen leaves and other plant matter. Fungi extract nutrients from the resulting humus and swap these nutrients with trees and plants around them. Some leaves take a long time to decompose, which allows animals such as toads and dormice to use piles of the leaves to shelter, hide and hibernate in.

As well as appreciating the beautiful shades of autumn leaves, this is an excellent time to admire the wide variety of leaf shapes. Some are long and pointed, some are round; some have smooth edges, some serrated. Look closely. You will find that not all leaves change shades in a uniform way. For example, the large green leaves of the horse chestnut tree are developing attractive, rusty patches. Admire these and then pick up a shiny conker from the ground.

Grey squirrel eating hawthorn berries.

The bushes in the hedgerow are full of bright berries: red ones on the hawthorn bush; bright pink and orange flower-shaped ones on the spindle; marble-sized blue-black ones (sloes) on the spiky blackthorn bush; juicy black and purple blackberries on the bramble; glossy red hips on the wild rose bush. The latter is dotted with a few mossy galls, known as robin's pincushions, which resemble hairy sweet chestnut balls. These contain larvae which have developed from eggs laid in the buds by gall wasps in spring. The larvae will consume the gall tissue during winter and emerge as adults next spring.

By the end of autumn, the majority of flowers will have shrivelled or fallen away, leaving structural stalks and seedheads in which ladybirds and other insects will hibernate. Teasels are particularly attractive, with heads covered in hundreds of spiny bracts, reminiscent of a hairbrush. They were once used in the textile industry to comb cloth and can treat Lyme disease and other conditions, including skin conditions.

Between the trees, bracken and ferns turn shades of orange and bronze and provide excellent cover for the woodland's animals. With everything browning, stinging nettles are one of the only plants that hold their green. In autumn, they produce their second round of flowers, which are appreciated by both bees and birds, who in return aid the prolific spread of these plants. And how great it is that they grow well nearly everywhere: numerous insects rely on them, and so they play an essential role in the woodland ecosystem. (See more in the 'Insects' section of the spring chapter.)

The seeds of the woodland plants are distributed in various ways. Some, such as shepherd's purse, peas and honesty, use an explosive action. As the seedheads ripen, tension builds until their outer coverings burst open, projecting the seeds some considerable distance. Others are moved to new places by the animals that consume them, and bristly or sticky ones hitch a ride on fur or hair.

Oak

Although there are many kinds of oak tree, the two common to our woodlands are the English oak, also known as the pedunculate oak, with acorns that hang from a stalk that comes off the twigs, and the Sessile oak, with acorns that have short stalks or none at all, growing straight from the twigs. The acorns, which are the tree's fruit, can be ground into an ersatz coffee, which was a common practice during wartime.

Oak trees also have galls caused by wasps, and these are easier to find now that the leaves have fallen away. Examples include oak apples (up to 4cm in diameter), the smaller oak marble gall (from which a sepia ink can be made – the same ink Leonardo da Vinci drew with and the *Magna Carta* was signed with) and oak knopper galls (deformed acorns that are knobby and spiky in form).

Hazel

On the hazel trees are hazelnuts, also known as cobnuts. If you inspect them closely, you will notice that some of the shells have been pierced by wood mice to get to the tasty kernels within, leaving holes that make the nuts look as if they are saying 'Oh!' or 'Ah!'

Hazel trees were amongst the first to colonise our land following the retreat of the last glacier, and were probably aided in their spread by the early human settlers, who would have eaten the hazelnuts as they travelled.

Elderberries

Elderberries hang in heavy, drooping clusters from the mythical elder tree (see the photo on page 99), which is hollow inside and therefore good for turning into pipes, flutes and beads. The rich, dark fruit should never be eaten raw, but cooked into a syrup that is extremely high in Vitamin C and good for sore throats. Another option is to infuse a generic supermarket gin with them, to make a tasty tipple to enjoy during the colder months.

Blackberries.

Haws, sloes, blackberries and rosehips

The hawthorn, which gives us such beautiful blossom in spring, now bears hard, red berries that are excellent when infused into gin or turned into an immune-boosting syrup. The blackthorn is studded with marble-sized blue-back sloes, arguably the best fruit to infuse in gin, imparting the perfect balance of sweet and tart flavours. Blackberries are a universally-recognised fruit and are one of the few that are a pleasure to eat raw. Growing on the bramble plant and ripening at the end of summer, they work really well in brandy and in crumbles alongside harvested apples. Shiny red rosehips can be transformed (with a lot of patience and hard work) into a jelly or syrup, as can guelder rose berries, although they are apparently less flavourful.

Lime

From the tall common lime (or linden) tree, petite round green fruit hang on stems from the tree's leaves. These can be ground up into a paste that has a similar taste to chocolate. In summer, the flowers that precede these fruits can be seeped in hot water to create a tea that's good for colds and flu, digestive complaints, anxiety and migraines, and they can be used in cosmetics such as mouthwash and bath lotion for a naturally fresh taste and scent.

Fragments of ancient lime woods, which originally extended over much of England and Wales, exist in counties such as Herefordshire, Suffolk and Norfolk. In times past, lovers would meet under lime trees, perhaps because of its heart-shaped leaves. As a wood, lime rarely warps, and so it is the perfect material to use for musical instruments.

Sweet chestnuts.

Sweet chestnut

In October, the tasty fruit of the sweet chestnut tree should be ready. Although visually similar to the shiny reddish-brown conkers of the horse chestnut tree, sweet chestnuts are smaller and packed, up to four at a time, within green balls covered in long, light green spikes rather than a smoother green shell covered in sharp points. The leaves of the sweet chestnut tree are long (the longest of all the woodland trees), shiny and dark green, with serrated edges, unlike the rounded, lighter green lobes of horse chestnut tree leaves. The bark of the tree often spirals around the trunk in deep grooves.

  After the challenge of opening the shells to get to the ripe fruit within, you can enjoy these tasty morsels roasted, candied, or in a soup.

Keys

The ash, birch, elm, field maple, Norway maple, sycamore and birch trees have winged fruit (known as 'keys') that aren't appetizing to humans. However, they will be nibbled by birds such as goldfinches. These seeds are spread in birds' droppings or by the winds that blow them spiralling away. You can tell field maple keys from sycamore and Norway maple keys, as the former are a more horizontal moustache shape than the others.

Beech mast

The oval leaves of the beech tree are shiny and smooth on top, with a wavy edge.

Clematis.

At this time of year, beech trees drop their seeds, which are miniature nuts surrounded by a prickly case. These are a favourite foodstuff of wild boar and pigs.

Clematis and mistletoe

Once the trees are finally empty of their leaves, you will be able observe where the climbing clematis is woven through the branches. The long, fluffy white hairs attached to the seeds give it its country name, 'old man's beard'. In the tops of some trees, you will be able to spot circular clumps of mistletoe. With leathery green leaves and pearlescent berries, mistletoe is fiercely guarded by the mistle thrush bird.

Ivy

In reverse to many other plants, ivy flowers in late autumn, providing rare and much-needed nectar for bees and wasps. These will develop into berries for the winter season.

THE SECRET LIFE OF A WOODLAND HABITAT

Mushrooms and fungi

While mushrooms – the fruiting bodies of certain fungi that reside underground (or in tree tissue) – actually appear throughout the year in the woodland, it's the damp and cool conditions in autumn that make them more abundant. The mulch of fallen leaves provides a fertile base for mushrooms that spread across the woodland floor. They are less hidden by the dense vegetation of spring and summer, and are enjoyed as a food source by squirrels, deer, rabbits, insects and some birds.

There are people out there who have enough expertise to forage for mushrooms, but in general it isn't worth taking the risk. Some might be edible; however, there are incredibly poisonous mushrooms that look almost identical to the safe ones. Further to that, it's much kinder to the environment to leave them where they are, to continue their valuable role within the woodland ecosystem.

This section covers some interesting examples to keep an eye out for.

Fly agaric

This is the mushroom that a lot people will recognise, even if they don't know its name or see it in real life. This ruby red fairy-tale toadstool of children's stories, including *Alice in Wonderland* (where she is given some to eat by the caterpillar), grows near to birch trees and conifers for a few precious weeks in October/November.

Jelly ear.

The pretty white spots that dapple this mushroom's cap (see the photo on the back cover) are in fact the remnants of torn-apart skin that originally covered the toadstool when it was just a small swelling coming from the earth. It is unlikely that you'll find a new and pristine fly agaric unless you're very lucky; they are usually quickly nibbled by animals. Don't be tempted to sample it yourself – it's toxic to humans!

Jelly ear

Jelly ear fungus generally grows on the bark of elder or beech trees. Weirdly wrinkled on one side and smoother on the other, and with a jelly texture, this bracket fungus grows in clusters up trees or across dead logs.

According to myth, it was the elder tree that Judas hung himself from, and so Christians believed that this fungus represented his tormented soul. Some particularly large specimens may remind you of the floppy ears of Roald Dahl's Big Friendly Giant. This creepy fungus proves that woodlands are always listening!

Dead man's fingers

Locate a rotting tree in a dank corner of the woodland and look closely. You might discover fingers coming out of it! Fear not, it isn't a dead body or a zombie: it's the dead man's fingers fungus. When young, this fungus is light grey in colour with a nail-like whitish tip. As it ages, it darkens to black. Therefore, should you find some, consider going back regularly to observe how they transform over the course of the fungus' lifecycle.

Candlesnuff fungus

You've got a good chance of finding candlesnuff fungus in a woodland, as it is very common. You just need to keep your eyes peeled, due to its diminutive size. Growing from dead tree stumps – often through moss – it is distinguished by its forked, antler shape. For this reason, another name given to it is stag's horn fungus. Black at the base, grey in the middle and white at the top, the fungus looks similar to a snuffed-out candle wick! This special fungus is used in medicine for its anti-viral and tumour-fighting properties.

Candlesnuff fungus.

Puffballs

Puffballs are soft, round mushrooms encrusted with tiny spikes (except for the giant puffball, which is smooth), that release spores from a hole in their top. When raindrops fall on this upper part, a puff of spores is released into the air, to land and grow further fruiting bodies elsewhere. Puffballs come in a variety of shades of whites, creams and browns. They are found nearly all year round and are amongst the easiest mushrooms to identify.

Witches' butter

Yellow brain fungus, also known as witches' butter, is a bizarre, irregularly shaped mass of orange/yellow that grows on dead wood, usually from oak or beech trees. It is slimy and gelatinous when wet, but harder when dry. This fungus is parasitic, feeding on the wood-rotting fungi of the *Peniophora* genus, eventually enveloping it completely. In folklore, it was said that if this fungus appeared on a house's door or gate, a witch had cast a spell on the family living there. The way to remove the spell was to pierce the fungus with pins until it went away. However, this fungus may not actually be a curse, as the compounds it produces have anti-inflammatory and anti-allergy properties.

King Alfred's cakes

At 2–10cms in diameter, these black clumps grow on dead wood – especially on ash and beech trees. Their name comes from the story that, while King Alfred hid from the Vikings in a peasant woman's house, he (after being asked to take care of the woman's cakes baking by the fire), fell asleep. These fungi are said to resemble the charred remains of those cakes. Another name for them is cramp balls, since it is said that they will cure a stitch or cramp if they are carried by the sufferer. Ancient people also used them as firelighters – a technique that goes all the way back to the Stone Age.

King Alfred's cakes.

Mycelium and trees

The roots of the fungi that grow beneath the woodland floor split into thread-like hyphae and form complex networks called mycelium. Through their colonies of mycelium, fungi absorb and digest nutrients from the soil. This breaks down the organic compounds of plants and animals, thus improving the soil and making nutrients and water easier to access for other plants and microorganisms. Through their mycelium, fungi can process toxins, removing pollutants from their environment. This benefits the ecosystem as a whole, making it healthier. In addition, structure is given to the soil and moisture is maintained. Multiple soil invertebrates rely on fungi and mycelium as a food source.

Mycelium have a close relationship with trees, attaching themselves to tree roots in order to swap nutrients. As they are unable to photosynthesise, mycelium take sugars from the trees and give nitrogen and phosphorus to them in return. Furthermore, an underground connection between the trees of the woodland is provided by mycelium, creating a familial bond and allowing strong trees to help suffering or dying trees by transporting nutrients to them through mycelium. Together, mycelium and trees play an essential role in removing carbon from the atmosphere, sequestering it within themselves and the soil.

When two compatible mycelia meet, they form a secondary mycelium which produces the fruiting bodies that we know as mushrooms or fungi. These mushrooms and fungi release spores which, when they land in a favourable position, will germinate and begin the process all over again.

Mycelium networks can spread for miles underground, with the largest recorded in Oregon, USA, at nearly 1,500 hectares wide and more than 2,000 years old.

Moss and lichen

Mosses grow on the ground and on trees and fallen logs in the woodland. They differ from flowering plants because they do not have true roots and they produce spores in order to spread. They reproduce in damp conditions by using a film of water to deliver the male cells to the female ones. This can happen within one plant, or between two, depending on the species. Mosses are home to invertebrates such as slugs and woodlice, which themselves become food for foraging birds and other animals. They soak up rainfall and add humidity to an environment.

One example includes ordinary moss (*Brachythecium rutabulum*) – a common moss in the UK – which is dark green and sometimes tinged with yellow, with branching stems that have pointed oval leaves that are toothed on the edges.

Lichens are also easier to spot on the branches and trunks of trees during this season. They come in a variety of greens, blues, oranges and yellows and in a range of textures and shapes, such as crusty spots, small standing branches and bushy beards. They are made up of an alga and/or cyanobacteria and a fungus existing in a mutually beneficial relationship: the algae/cyanobacteria carrying out photosynthesis to feed the fungus, and the fungus providing it with shelter. They grow slowly, by 1–2mm per year, and so are prevalent and extensive in undisturbed, ancient woodlands. They provide food and shelter for invertebrates and are gathered by many birds for their nest-making in spring.

As lichens are sensitive to pollution, the presence of them indicates the quality of the air in the environment and therefore the health of the woodland that they are in. For example, the crusty lichens can cope with higher levels of pollution, while the beardy ones only grow in the least-polluted woodlands. Ash trees are particularly important to lichens, as their highly alkaline bark can host up to 536 species.

Examples of lichens you can see include the yellow scale, or common orange lichen (*Xanthoria parietina*), which varies in shades of yellow and orange and can even appear grey-green in the shade. It is frequently found on elder trees.

Physcia adscendens *lichen*.

Physcia adscendens is a pale grey lichen with swollen, hood-shaped lobes. Widespread in the UK, it is one of the lichens that is fairly tolerant of nitrogen pollution.

Cup lichen (*Cladonia fimbriata*) has trumpet-shaped fruiting bodies that are 3–4cm in height and grow on logs, tree roots and on the ground.

Mosses and lichens are non-parasitic and do not harm the trees they grow on.

Birds

At this time of year, lots of birds leave the UK for the warmer climes of places such as Africa and Spain, but others, such as redwings and fieldfares, begin to arrive.

From the end of summer and through autumn, starlings arrive from elsewhere in Europe, such as Scandinavia, the Baltic States and Russia, to join our resident starling population.

It is also in autumn that you have a good chance of finding feathers on the ground – a wood pigeon's scattered feathers after losing a battle with a predator, a lone jay feather, lost buzzard feathers, and iridescent magpie tail-feathers.

Pheasants call from deep within the woodland, trying to stay out of sight during an incredibly dangerous time for them (hunting season is from 1 October to 1 February).

Robins

While many other birds leave our shores, our resident robins hang around. In addition, they are joined by robins from other European countries. This is why, suddenly, robins seem to be everywhere – as if singing from every tree and hedge.

Their lovely, fluty song is now easily heard, since it is no longer being drowned out by other birdsong. Now that they can take centre stage, they make the most of it, filling the woodland with their voice. If you listen, you should hear one robin answering another. They are especially sensitive to light levels, and so are often the first and last bird to sing each day.

These friendly birds are anything but shy, and this is perhaps because they know that they have nothing to fear from us. And it is not unusual for them to provide you with sweet company while you walk. This is a behaviour that harks back to the days when they followed native wild boar around the woodland, picking up worms from the disturbed soil.

They are, however, feisty and aggressive with their fellow robins, as well as with other birds, to make sure that they get their fair share of food and territory, despite their diminutive size. They mainly eat earthworms,

Robin.

grubs, centipedes and other insects, as well as small berries. Unlike the majority of other birds, both the male and female robin sing, guard their own territories and have the same vibrant redbreast (although the male's can be brighter than the female's).

According to old country superstition, it is unlucky to injure or kill a robin, or to damage its nest, or break or steal its eggs. Harm a robin and you will be similarly harmed; interfere with its nest or eggs and you will experience misfortune afterwards. Luckily, this is unlikely, as robins are generally considered Britain's favourite bird. The robin is also linked to religion in various legends, one being that the bird's breast turned red after being stained with Christ's blood after trying to pull out a thorn from Christ's Crown of Thorns.

Since Victorian times, robins have been depicted on Christmas cards. This is a tradition that continues to this day.

Jays

As they prefer to stay hidden from human view, jays are easier to hear than see. It is the jay's harsh, screeching alarm call that will alert you to its presence. Cast your eyes quickly in the direction of the sound and you might spot this colourful corvid amongst the branches. Its pinkish-brown body is impressively camouflaged against bark lit up by the warm glow of the sun. However, keep looking and you will notice the distinctive electric-blue barring on its forewings' feathers, the moustachioed face and intelligent eye with its big black pupil, which

Jay.

confirms you have definitely located a jay. Once you have it in your sights, you can follow the jay's movements as it flies short distances from branch to branch and from tree to tree.

There are surprisingly few references to jays in folklore, despite the bird's intriguing habits and personality, and the charming combination of colours it possesses. Conversely, other members of the corvid family, such as crows and magpies, have a lot of myth and folklore attached to them. Maybe this is because jays are shy and therefore seen less often. However, the bird does have the Celtic name of '*schreachag choille*', meaning 'screamer of the woods'. This is probably due to the fact that, along with the blackbird, the jay is one of the chief alarmists of the woodland – warning the other creatures when danger, or a nosey human, is on its way. Mistrustful of our species (no doubt owing to a long history of persecution), the jay can nonetheless become quite fearless when entering gardens that border woodlands, where it fills its capacious throat-pouch with fruit, vegetables and food from the bird-table. Usually, its diet consists of invertebrates and nuts from the woodland environment.

'Planter of the woodlands' would be an apt name for the jay. Its habit of gathering, storing and sometimes forgetting nuts such as acorns and beech mast results in the growth of new trees, especially oaks. In fact, it is believed that jays can be credited for the rapid spread of oak trees following the last Ice Age – which, since jays have been recorded carrying single acorns as far as 20km, is believable. Each autumn, these industrious birds can bury as many as 5,000 acorns, thus helping to plant the grand old trees of the future. Since they are busy collecting nuts for their cache, you have a better chance of seeing jays during autumn.

Unfortunately, the jay has become vulnerable to urban spread, with human dwellings encroaching and taking over its woodland habitat. While those living in urban areas are therefore increasingly able to see jays, it also means that these handsome birds are more at risk of decline.

Redwings and fieldfares

From October onwards, flocks of redwings and fieldfares arrive to forage for food in our woodlands and hedges, gobbling up whole trees' worth of ruby berries. The seeds of these fruits will be spread across a wide area, deposited in the birds' droppings as they travel around the woodland.

Redwings.

Redwings also scratch and peck the ground for worms and insects and, as this forms the majority of their diet, they can starve if there is a thick layer of snow on the ground.

Being fairly similar-looking birds, both with speckled breasts, one way to tell a redwing from a fieldfare is by the red blush under the former's wing (hence the name). The fieldfare is larger than the redwing and can be distinguished by its grey head and rump.

Despite safety in numbers, these birds are easily disturbed by a wandering human, and will quickly burst out of their feeding areas and fly away. They will leave the UK in March.

Pheasants

Pheasants were introduced to England from the East in the eleventh century, and then later to Ireland, Wales and Scotland. These large birds, with their long, elegant tails, will browse the woodland floor for food such as seeds, berries and insect larvae during the day, and roost in trees to avoid predators (such as foxes) at night.

They need to be wary of hunters during autumn and winter, which probably explains why they are spooked when you come across them. They will tend to keep out of your way, with the multi-hued male's harsh 'koork-kok' call – that echoes through the woodland – being the only sign that they are about.

Male pheasant.

Insects

The last of summer's insects source nectar from the late-blooming flowers.

Amongst the white dead-nettle plants, you might come across an exhausted queen bee taking deep draughts of nectar (see the photo on page 13). She is either preparing to hibernate before building her nest in spring, or will begin her work in autumn (an increasing trend amongst the bees in southern UK).

Certain butterflies, such as the peacock, small tortoiseshell and comma, as well as some moths, will seek a sheltered place amongst ivy and other foliage, where they will stay in a state of torpor during winter. Ladybirds and other beetles will nestle amongst the leaf litter, in the dried heads of plants such as teasels, and in the fissures of tree bark. Snails will seal themselves into their shells with their slime and will huddle in a sheltered area until spring returns.

Other insects will die off, but not before leaving their legacy in egg or larvae form to hatch and develop the following spring.

By the end of autumn, flies will have crawled into cracks to overwinter, although they may reappear on sunny days. They will wake up in spring to lay their eggs on decaying matter.

Mammals

Squirrels
Squirrels are busy gathering thousands of fallen acorns and other nuts. Red squirrels, who prefer to stay up in the trees – more so than their grey counterparts – will risk foraging on the woodland floor for this precious bounty.

Grey squirrel eating a nut.

While eating as much as they can to build up their fat reserves for winter, they will also bury many across the woodland floor and in other suitable places, such as holes in trees. This cache will provide them with a larder they can dip into throughout the leaner winter months. Although red squirrels have excellent spatial memories and grey squirrels can locate most of their nuts using their excellent sense of smell, some nuts are inevitably forgotten or lost. Rather than being consumed, these nuts instead have the opportunity to become the woodland's new saplings. In this way, squirrels provide a wonderful dispersal and planting service for trees, ensuring the regeneration of the woodland as a whole.

Deer

Autumn is a dramatic time for the UK's largest land mammals. Charged with hormones, male red deer compete with one another to assert their dominance and to access females to mate with. This is known as the 'rut', and it occurs from the end of September to November. With clashing antlers and roaring in the woodlands, these battles can mean life or death for the deer or, at the very least, whether their genes are passed on. Although sexually mature by the time they are two years old, stags don't tend to mate until they are five years old. It is at this time that the sexes mix, spending the rest of the year apart. In the woodland environment, red deer are largely solitary, with the exception of mother and calf groups.

There is, however, one deer species in the UK that does not have a 'rut': the muntjac. Instead of having a defined breeding season like other deer species, muntjac deer breed all year round.

Hedgehogs

Sheltering in nests made of grass, moss and fallen leaves, hedgehogs will hibernate from November to March. To do this, they drop their temperature to match their surroundings. If autumn or winter is mild, hedgehogs may remain active for longer. Once in hibernation, hedgehogs will use up the fat stores that they developed during summer.

The loss of woodland and hedgerow habitats means that, with less food and shelter available to them, the number of hedgehogs has decreased massively.

Badgers

During autumn, badgers will forage furiously on the woodland's numerous resources to develop a thick layer of fat under their skin. This will give them reserves to live off during winter, when they spend much of their time underground and feed less.

Foxes

From late September, most if not all of the fox cubs – who were born between March and May of the previous year – will leave the family unit. They are now fully self-sufficient and independent enough to disperse to establish their own territories. The females that stay with the family may help to bring up next year's cubs. The cubs are now indistinguishable from the adults in terms of their looks.

Bats

At the beginning of autumn, male bats are productive in the time left to them before they need to hibernate. They will emit special clicks, purrs and buzzing calls to attract the females. Male pipistrelles, for example, will display for the benefit of passing females from the temporary mating roosts they set up in trees at the end of summer.

Fox.

During this mating season, both genders will increase their stores of fat to help them survive the coldest months, and seek out hibernation sites in old trees. In October, although mating is still continuing, the cooler weather means that bats will start to enter periods of torpor. (Torpor is a sleep-like state in which the bats' body temperatures and metabolic rates decrease.) By November these periods will increase in length until, one by one, the bats enter full hibernation for winter.

THE SECRET LIFE OF A WOODLAND HABITAT

Woodland conservation

Now that you know a little (or a lot) more about your local woodlands, you'll want to find out how protect them, as well as what is being done across the UK to save these unique environments and their varied wildlife – from new woodland creation to animal reintroductions. This chapter covers relevant projects, campaigns and governmental promises at the time of writing in 2021. Hopefully, by the time you read this, many of the steps required to restore our natural world will have already been taken.

The state of our woodlands

Shockingly, as revealed in the Woodland Trust's 'State of the UK's Woods and Trees 2021' report, only 7% of our native British woodland can be considered in 'good' ecological condition. This means that not only should we plant new trees and woodland, but we must ensure that they are of a good ecological condition, and that our existing woodlands are cared for and improved.

One main factor that leads to the report's analysis is the lack of dead wood that can be found in these places. It is all too easy to assume that, once a tree is dead, it no longer serves a purpose. However, as explained in several places within this book, dead wood is an essential habitat and food source for numerous species. It also provides the service of returning vital nutrients to the soil, which get reused by other plants, trees and fungi, thus contributing to their overall health. In turn, this benefits the species that rely on them, and so the woodland as a whole thrives. Another issue found by the report is that there aren't enough old, veteran trees present in our woodlands. Again, these provide an ecological niche for various woodland species.

Non-native conifer plantations do not have a variety of native tree species, nor an assortment of ages of trees – due to the trees being planted at the same time – and so they do not meet the ideal state for excellent biodiversity. And yet, none of the native woodlands exceed 19% in favourable condition for age distribution of trees either.

Careful woodland management is needed to develop the range of ages and species of trees in our woodlands and to provide the structural diversity necessary for better ecological conditions. Woodland management must be balanced, allowing old trees to stand and dead wood to stay where it is, while coppicing other trees to prolong their lives, felling some to allow room for other species, and managing certain areas to create or maintain open spaces, while allowing an abundance of natural regeneration. Furthermore, if we do this, our woodlands will become resilient against the impact of climate change, pests and diseases.

Our existing woodlands also appear as isolated patches across intensely-managed agricultural land, as well as between and around built-up regions of human dwellings. The report emphasises the importance of connecting up our woodland habitats, so that wildlife can safely move between them. This will aid the survival of species due to enhanced opportunities to forage, shelter and find mates, the latter ensuring a healthy flow of genes within species.

Coppiced hazel stems gathered together for various uses.

The report also states that we should continually monitor these spaces against required objectives, adapting them where necessary, to make sure that management and conservation methods are having the desired effect of improving the condition and resilience of our woodlands.

Trees are amongst our best weapons against climate change, the report confirms, in the way they remove carbon dioxide from the atmosphere. It is believed that 77 million tonnes of carbon is currently being stored just by our ancient and long-established woodlands across England, Scotland and Wales, with the total store of carbon by *all* of our forests and woodlands being estimated at 213 million tonnes. This shows how important it is that we protect and extend our existing woodlands, as well as creating new ones. The report's results showed that the best carbon storers are the native, broadleaved trees: oak came top, followed by beech, ash then birch. It is worth remembering that these figures will only rise as younger trees age: the older trees are, the better their sequestering abilities.

The Woodland Trust supports the Committee on Climate Change's proposed target of increasing the UK's woodland cover from 13% to 19% by 2050. This is more ambitious than the government's aim of merely increasing England's tree cover from 10% to 12% by 2060.

Green woodland.

The Woodland Trust is one of the organisations that has pushed the government to set legally-binding targets as part of the Environment Act, to make sure that necessary action is taken across the country.

Planting new woodlands

There have been many planting campaigns over the years, organised by community groups and organisations, to increase tree cover across the UK.

A recent example includes the Woodland Trust's Big Climate Fightback Campaign, launched in 2021. The aim of the project is to plant 50 million trees over a period of 5 years, to ensure that there are enough of our arboreal heroes to meet the UK Government's target of being carbon net zero by 2050.

In 2018, the UK Government published a policy paper entitled 'A Green Future: Our 25 Year Plan to Improve the Environment'. To bring about signification changes within a generation, one thing they promise to do is plant 180,000 hectares by the end of 2042, to increase England's woodland cover to 12% by 2060. They say they will also protect and enhance natural spaces and encourage people to spend time in them to reap the benefits for their health and well-being.

They assure us that they will also reach the goals set out in 2018's 'Tree Health Resilience Plan', which describes strategies such as establishing stringent biosecurity methods to safeguard England's trees from the threats they face from disease and pests.

Heartwood Forest

Heartwood Forest in St Albans, Hertfordshire, is an exemplary illustration of how converting agricultural land back to woodland brings about beneficial changes. Between 2009 and 2019, volunteers there planted 600,000 trees. By doing this and also creating an eclectic mix of habitats, what was previously a nature-depleted area is becoming richer with wildlife every year. The existing pockets of ancient woodland are being linked with new planting and hedgerows, to both expand tree cover and provide wildlife with much-needed nature corridors.

The results of the data which have been recorded by Heartwood's wildlife monitors since the beginning of the project are clear: the conservation efforts have boosted biodiversity considerably. For example, the number of birds at Heartwood has grown by 44% over the ten years. One individual species – the whitethroat – has experienced a tripling of its numbers. Over the same time period, butterfly numbers have gone up by a whopping 300%.

Future plans at the site are to maintain the ancient woodlands through coppicing and other woodland management techniques. This will prolong the life of the trees, and ensure that there is an assortment of ages

Whitethroat at Heartwood Forest.

and stages of growth. Dead wood will also be left in place to break down. These factors will make for a healthy and resilient woodland that supports a diverse and multifaceted ecosystem.

As the woodlands grow and develop at Heartwood, the 858-acre site will only become increasingly efficient at capturing and locking away carbon from the atmosphere, directly fighting against climate change.

Reintroductions and rewilding

There have also been admirable and note-worthy schemes to reintroduce several of our lost animal species. Stunning red kites have been restored to our skies, especially in Southeast England; golden and white-tailed eagles are returning to their Scottish haunts; white storks are breeding again in Sussex. Wild boar are snuffling through forests in Kent; beavers are reworking the rivers in Devon and beyond; and there is talk of bringing back wolves, bears and lynxes across the UK.

In 'A Green Future' the government promised to work to prevent future extinction of our animal species (including the threatened curlew), and to continue to reintroduce species where they are missing. It plans to restore wildlife habitats and address the issues facing our wildflowers and pollinators.

Knepp Estate

Based in West Sussex, Knepp Estate was also once farmland, until the farmers decided to do something wholly unprecedented in the UK: they gave the land back to nature.

Adopting a low-maintenance ethos, Knepp's guardians are allowing the landscape to regenerate itself, with the addition of free-roaming long-horned cattle, Exmoor ponies and Tamworth pigs (see pages 94 and 95) to

Exmoor ponies at Knepp Estate.

provide a low-impact grazing service. The impressive site is now a mosaic of woodland and heathland that hosts a wide range of species.

One result of this rewilding is that sallow (willow) shoots have sprung up where the pigs have rootled, leading to a boom in purple emperor butterfly numbers, who lay their eggs on this plant. The red-listed turtle dove (see pages 78 and 79) and long-declining nightingale, as well as herds of deer, have found a sanctuary at Knepp. It is also the location of the White Stork Project, where the first wild white stork chicks in England for 600 years hatched in May 2020.

Conclusion

With raised awareness of the plight of our degraded natural world, and valiant efforts being made across the UK to turn the tide, the environment is now very much on the national agenda. But we cannot take change for granted; there is still a long way to go. People are therefore speaking up to spread the message further, and to apply pressure on our government. Many are also joining initiatives and supporting charities to improve the situation. Why not be one of them?

Fallow stag at Knepp Estate.

How to help woodlands and wildlife

1. Join your local Wildlife Trust or Woodland Trust group, or another conservation charity group, to help maintain and conserve your local woodland and wildlife.

2. Become a citizen scientist! In these climate-change times, it's vital to have data to track the changes taking place in terms of the timings of nature events, such as the appearance of the first wildflowers of the year, as well as the numbers of species in your area. There are lots of schemes, including the Botanical Society of Britain and Ireland (BSBI)'s New Year Plant Hunt and the Woodland Trust's Nature Calendar. These schemes are also another way to become familiar with your local woodland!

3. Sign petitions to protect woodlands and green spaces local to you, and also nationwide. Contact your local MP to let them know your environmental concerns.

4. Help to stop trees from being cut down and plant more trees!

5. Let your garden grow wild! This helps insects, and therefore all animals.

6. Educate yourself about tree pests and diseases, and report any signs of these in your local woodland and area. See further information on reporting at **www.gov.uk/guidance/report-a-tree-pest-or-disease-overview**

7. Be vocal and speak to your friends, family and local community about the issues our environment and world is facing, encouraging them to make positive lifestyle changes. You could even buy them a copy of this book, to guide them into the wonderful world of woodlands and wildlife!

Resources

Books

Blamey, M., Fitter, R. and Fitter, A. *Wild Flowers of Britain & Ireland.* A & C Black.
Burton, M. *Wild Mammals of the British Isles.* Frederick Warne & Co, Ltd.
Cooper, A. *Watching Wildlife.* Usborne Pocket Naturalist.
Hume, R. *Birds of Britain and Europe.* Dorling Kindersley.
Humphries, C.J. *Wildflowers.* Usborne Spotter's Guides.
Johnson, O. and More, D. *Tree Guide.* HarperCollins.
Rackham, O. *Woodlands.* HarperCollins.
Radford, E. and M.A., Hole, C. (ed.). *Superstitions of the Countryside.* Arrow Books.
White, Gilbert. *The Natural History of Selborne.* Oxford University Press.
Wilkinson, J. and Tweedie, M. *Handguide to the Butterflies and Moths of Britain and Europe.* Collins.
Woolf, J. *Britain's Trees: A Treasury of Traditions, Superstitions, Remedies and Literature.* National Trust.
The Ever-changing Woodlands. Reader's Digest.

Websites

A Green Future: Our 25 Year Plan to Improve the Environment: www.gov.uk/government/publications/25-year-environment-plan

Tree health resilience strategy 2018: www.gov.uk/government/publications/tree-health-resilience-strategy-2018

State of the UK's Woods and Trees 2021: woodlandtrust.org.uk/state-of-uk-woods-and-trees/

Botanical Society of Britain and Ireland (BSBI)'s New Year Plant Hunt: https://nyph.bsbi.org/take-part

The British Deer Society (BDS): bds.org.uk

British Trust for Ornithology (BTO): bto.org

Buglife: buglife.org.uk

Bumblebee Conservation Trust: bumblebeeconservation.org

Butterfly Conservation: butterfly-conservation.org

Knepp Wildland: https://knepp.co.uk/home

The Mammal Society: mammal.org.uk

Plantlife: plantlife.org.uk

Reporting signs of tree pests and diseases: www.gov.uk/guidance/report-a-tree-pest-or-disease-overview

The Royal Society for the Protection of Birds (RSPB): rspb.org.uk (bird ID guides, with birdsong, can be found here)

The Wildlife Trusts (find your local group, wildlife events, etc.): wildlifetrusts.org

Woodland Trust (see more about their Big Climate Fightback Campaign, how to get involved, other initiatives, tree ID guide): woodlandtrust.org.uk

The Woodland Trust's Nature's Calendar: naturescalendar.woodlandtrust.org.uk

Index

N.B. Numbers in **bold** indicate a relevant photo on that page.